A STRUCTURED PRAYER MANUAL FOR WOMEN

MUMS' ALTAR

DR. OMOBOLA JEFFREYS

Dr. Omobola Jeffreys' Book
Published by Homotayor Creativity World

All rights reserved.
No part of this publication may be reproduced, stored in a retrieval system or transmitted in any form or by any means, electronic, mechanical, photocopying, recording or otherwise without prior written permission of the publisher.

The only exception is brief quotation in printed reviews.
Most bible quotations are taken from
The Holy Bible King James version,
unless otherwise stated.

FOREWORD

MUMS' ALTAR Altar is practical and useful prayer tool. With content focused on motherhood, the prayer points are well defined, and scripturally designed to deal with the root cause of whatever issues the reader is praying about. Reading through, the book is broken into simple categories and headings to help the readers follow along. The prayer points are geared towards satisfying the prayer needs of many readers.

This prayer guide is riveting with Dr. Omobola Jeffreys giving prayer a new easy and interesting dimension. I must add also that this guidebook is not just for women; it is for anyone, male or female, who wants to pray, the young and the old alike.

D R N Jeffreys
March 2020

TABLE OF CONTENTS

CHAPTER 1	PROSPERITY	// 05
CHAPTER 2	FAVOUR	// 19
CHAPTER 3	PEACE	// 37
CHAPTER 4	LOCATION	// 54
CHAPTER 5	SALVATION	// 74
CHAPTER 6	SAFETY	// 90
CHAPTER 7	REST AND REWARD	// 102
CHAPTER 8	MOTHER HELPED BY GOD	// 109
CHAPTER 9	MERCY	// 128

Acknowledgement

My children have challenged me to be the best parent that I could be. The desire to support them, the desire to see them excel has been the reason for warring on my knees in the place of prayer. To the great destinies that God has handed to me for care-taking, I owe a duty of care.

This book is dedicated to every woman who is committed to birthing great destinies in the place of prayer.

May your joy be full and your reward lasting as you partner with God in moulding these destinies.

To my husband, Pastor Dumebi Jeffreys, for covering and co-labouring with me, I am grateful for your leadership.

— 05 —

Chapter 1
PROSPERITY

INTRODUCTION

Mothers are good at nurturing destinies; this is a God given ability which when ignored can lead to immature and sometimes dead destinies. This is commendable, however, to start off this delightful journey; in this session, you will be praying for yourself so that you can be able to stand fit and proper to fulfil this God given commission.

It is important to God that we prosper as mothers; I want to share a story with you; a story a lot of you are conversant with; the story of the wife of the sons of the prophet.

> ***2 Kings Chapter 4:1-2 (NIV)***
> *1. The wife of a man from the company of the prophets cried out to Elisha, "Your servant my husband is dead, and you know that he revered the Lord. But now his creditor is coming to take my two boys as his slaves."*
> *2. Elisha replied to her, "How can I help you? Tell me, what do you have in your house? "Your servant has nothing there at all," she said, "except a small jar of olive oil."*

This story upsets me almost every time I read it; observing the way this story is told in the bible, this was a man who was dedicated to the work of the master, who was persistently in the house of the Lord, who was serving, who was following the prophet, who was also committed to the work of the ministry and was doing a tangible work with the master. As we have been told that God blesses us when we serve him; We have been taught that God honours us beautifully when we give our time to him. Yet we did not see such a proof in the life of this man! His story clarified an essential truth that in spite of the fact that we serve, we do so ignorantly at times. God expects us to use our brain to acquire resources that will keep us enriched and our needs met, rather than being idle and just claiming that we are serving God.

With the lesson from this story, I hope that as we spend time to pray, the Lord will open our eyes, as women to know how to handle our homes and how to support our husbands to make right choices regarding what they need to do, to generate funds needed to take care of our needs and leave a good inheritance for our children.

We are regularly taught to give our husband to the Lord, that prosperity will come to us once we do so; but the story we've read in this scripture does not confirm that at all. The scripture reveals to us that the man in the scripture made a mistake. He was busy but not planning for his future. A lot of people are making the similar mistake.

In the same vein, a common mistake we make as Christian women is the assumption that we will live anyhow we choose; but pass on the responsibility to the magical God who will sort everything out. That is not right. We need to plan for the responsibility which we have acquired through parenting.

My husband says that "if you want to know what you can afford, the life you can live, look in your statement of account, look in your pocket, see what is available there. There is no need to live above your means, buying things you cannot afford on credit. You will be saying some prayers which some women will find difficult, you are going to be praying that the Lord will make you live responsibly , no matter how difficult it is for your taste and lifestyle.

How can God trust you with great wealth when you invest all you have in short term pleasures? You must be accountable for the wealth God has been committed to you. Some women are running into debts because of greed, and they start praying, for God to cover or cancel their debts. A woman who has gone into debt because material things instead of solid investments is not a wise woman . God will not rescue you from the consequences of a greedy lifestyle.

It is cruelty towards your children if you live your life as though the future does not exist. One of the responsibilities that the Lord has given you as parents is to provide for your children, and to take care of their future.

The bible says that the godly man leaves an inheritance for his children *(Proverbs 13:22)* - how can you leave an inheritance when you are living in debt every day?

How can you leave inheritance when you have put no inheritance away? It doesn't matter what has happened so far, tonight, you will be praying as mothers who now has insight and know better.

PRAYER POINTS

1. Ask the Lord to bless the labour of your hands and sweat.
2. Not all labours are profitable. Receive a profitable labour in the mighty name of Jesus.
3. Father, you will enable me to make the right assessment and judgement regarding that which will make my sweat profitable and make my hands prosperous.
4. Ask the Lord to enable you to make riches and great wealth in the mighty name of Jesus.
5. The bible says **in Deuteronomy 8:18** "it is You Lord who gives us power to make wealth" ask the Father in the name of Jesus, for heaven to enable you to explore all that is needed for you to enjoy which heaven has already approved of. Receive great success in your ventures; receive power to make rewarding works in the mighty name of Jesus
6. The bible says in **John 3:27** that no man receives anything except they be given from above, ask the Father in the name of Jesus, lay hold on his promises, receive the power to excel and prosper in the works your hand in the mighty name of Jesus.

7. Receive the power to subdue mountains financially, in the mighty name of Jesus.
8. Ask the Father to reveal profitable business ventures, righteous ideas; receive tonight the ability to discern profitable and non-profitable ones.
9. Receive insight and perseverance that will help you commit to that which will yield great results for you in the name of Jesus.
10. Command from today, wealth in the name of Jesus, through the labour of my hands, through your sweat and many gifts that shall be given to you in the mighty name of Jesus
11. Decree that you are a prosperous woman, in the work your hands and in the results which you acquire through your skills.
12. Receive also the reputation for sufficiency and enough to bless many.
13. Decree that you will not make stupid choices regarding that which was scheduled to enrich you. You will go out and you will prosper in the mighty name of Jesus.

Some people manage millions worth of investment without stepping out of the doors of their house. You will now pray:
14. Ask the Lord to give you the wisdom it takes to claim financial grounds in the name of Jesus.

The bible encourages us to bring our strong reasons...
15. Tell the Lord that you need this to be able to take care of your family and all the responsibilities God has given you in the mighty name of Jesus.

This same prophet's wife was probably happy and was being addressed as mummy prophet, a title which may have given her a false sense of security - we know people like her. There may have been many people who did everything for her. She may have had sisters who cleaned the house, ones who helped with the shopping, sister who did the laundry and the ones allocated to pick the children from school!!!

She may have just sat back, enjoying a grandiose air, after all, she deserved it. Her husband was serving. Not enriching yourself, not enriching other people, as a result of a temporary position you occupy - *that is stupidity of the highest order.* If you're a pastor's wife and all you do is just wait for people to serve you whilst your husband ministers to them; lazily enjoying pastor's wife's privileges, you're deliberately bringing and inviting insult to yourself from the people.

A lot of women do not step out because they don't know who they are and what they are made of. There are many gifts inside you that you're sometimes not aware of.

At a meeting in Nigeria in January 2016, one of the ladies who attended the meeting gave us a feedback. She said that as she sat down and listened, she noted everything that was said and when she got back home that night, she decided that she was going to action all that she had heard. This woman had learnt how to make kunu - a delicious Nigerian yoghurt. That was a skill she had acquired long before the conference. Being employed by the local government, her salaries were few and far between. With irregular payments, the income was insufficient for her young family. Following the counsel from the conference, she decided to start a business making the yoghurt drink for public consumption. Before we left her city, her husband contacted us and reported how she took it to work and sold everything and she had money to hand.

Do you think her family will go hungry that night? No.

You're going to pray now:
16. Father, open my eyes to see what you have deposited in me, that will empower me to command riches.
17. Lord to open your eyes to see the gifting that is scheduled to release me into financial freedom.
18. Father help me to unravel the great mystery of prosperity in me, that I will not labor and struggle while many are struggling.

19. Father even when people say that there is a letting down, that there is a cloud that is not shifting, I will say that there is prosperity, because my efforts will be blessed.
20. Father celebrate and advertise me, every gift you've put inside of me can become great through your advertisement.
21. Father I receive full access to prosperity, to make use of that which you've deposited in me Lord because within me is the ability to excel.
22. I receive direction and the activation of all that you have put inside of me that they will not be wasted in the name of Jesus.
23. Father I tap into the ability to make money, to acquire wealth, in a godly and profitable manner. I receive the wisdom to actualise this in the name of Jesus.
24. Push forward and say, Lord, I gain understanding of godly means of prosperity recovery and I call forth riches right now through godly means even to my household, my husband, to my children. In the name of Jesus.

The bible says you should bring forth your strong reasons in Isaiah 14:21; I know that the reason I cannot be poor is that God has given me responsibilities. I hope you know that you can bring that before God. When God gives you children, you are partnering with God to raise those children, to give those children a means of livelihood.

You're going to pray today regarding the partnership that you have with God.
Speak to God and say
25. Father, I am a partner with you in this business of raising great destinies. For this reason,
    I cannot lack the things I need.
    I cannot lack whatever my children need.
    I cannot lack anything my husband needs.
    Lord, I ask that everything I need to raise my children, to make them comfortable, to give them the good things in life, Heaven release

them unto me right now and I receive them in Jesus name.
26. *Father, as the bible says – "money answers all things", I receive the money to take care of my family, to send my children to school, set them up in business endeavours that will enrich them for life, Father I receive these in the name of Jesus.*
27. *Father, for every monetary need we have as a family, we receive speedy answers in the mighty name of Jesus.*
28. *Lord, whether I know the way or not, I'm asking that you'll hand me over to people who will direct me. People who will connect me and direct me to where I need to be to make profit financially.*
29. *Father connect me with people who have insight regarding my journey to a abundance, so that I can apply myself unto prosperity in the name of Jesus.*
30. *Father, please hold me by the hand and hand me over to people who will support me, people who will teach me, people who will equip me, in the name of Jesus.*

Some of us are sitting on great wealth without knowing; some of these inheritances belonging to us have been taken away yet, we are still not aware.

Pray now and say:
31. *Lord every inheritance, monetary inheritance, inheritance of wealth that belongs to me that is lying in the hands of others, in the name of Jesus, I forcefully take them away from them. I recover all, in the name of Jesus.*
32. *Today, I pursue, I overtake and I recover all in the name of Jesus, every blessing that is due me, that is in the hands of others, in the name of Jesus I recover them.*

As we read in 2 Kings chapter 4, there was no difference between that prophet and somebody who did not know the Lord - that is not what the bible promised us.

Malachi Chapter 3:18 (NIV)
And you will again see the distinction between the righteous and the wicked, between those who serve God and those who do not.

Sincerely, prosperity should be ours, when people see how well we are doing, they should look at us and say, can you please show me the secret of your wealth and we should be pointing them to the cross. We should be saying when I met Jesus, He turned my life around. Not that people are looking at us and all they see is abject poverty around the children of God.

33. Father, according to your word, I receive all that it takes to make a difference between my camp and the camp of those who do not serve you.
34. I will not labour unduly, I will not struggle before I have access to that which is made for me in the name of Jesus.
35. Father from today, I will not beg, I will not lack, in the name of Jesus. Money will answer to me as I demand in the mighty name of Jesus.
36. I decree in the mighty name of Jesus, I am laying hold on that belongs to me, the Lord has told me, He said there will be a difference between those who do not serve and those who serve God, because I am righteous and I make my money through righteousness, prosperity is mine.
37. I am retaining wealth, wealth is not leaving me, I am not wasting my resources. I make commitment to profitable business, to profitable ventures, in the mighty name of Jesus.
38. I am spreading my wings and prospering all sides, in the name of Jesus.

For this so-called prophet, a man of God, there was no difference between him and those who didn't know the Lord. You're going to pray for your husband and household.

39. Because I am righteous and I serve you, there must be a difference between my household and those who do not honor the statues of your word. For this reason, i welcome a visible difference confirming my allegiance to you Lord.
40. In the mighty name of Jesus, I am prosperous in everything I put my labour into; they bring forth great results. My household is excelling in every business venture, even in the work of our hands, and all that we do.
41. I make profit in the morning as I wake and at night as I sleep. I make profits because God gives me idea that makes profit in Jesus name.

A while ago, we were praying for our children and we asked the Lord to give our children ideas that makes money. We prayed for our husbands, that the Lord will give our husbands lucrative ideas, big and relevant that the world has no choice but to honour them and give them due reward for such ideas.

You will pray same today:
42. I pray for unique ideas that nobody has ever thought about, profitable money-making ideas, Father, i ask that you allocate these to my household.
43. I receive direction, clear instruction in the name of Jesus regarding how to implement supernatural ideas.
44. Persistently, i will receive clear update and information in my sleep and in my subconscious. Lord, you will show me, in broad daylight you will open my eyes to see all that I need to see without holding back.
45. I pray, in the night, you will release to me great ideas that are profitable in the mighty name of Jesus. Through righteous means, my household is excelling in every way, we are taking territories, in Jesus name.

Brethren, I do not want to be a woman without power, a woman who has no money has no power, that is the truth. An ungodly husband will talk to you anyhow; neighbors will talk to you anyhow because you are going to ask them for food. You will be subject to people's opinion about your life. Everybody will disrespect you. When you have power, financial power, when you stand, you distinguish yourself. You are free to live to the best of God's purpose.

Poverty is a handicap. You need to break free from it, otherwise, it will ruin you.

Pray and say:
46. Father, I am a help meet for my husband. I am not a liability, make me a worthy support for my husband, empower me to be a worthy support, that whatever I need to release to my household, it will come to me easily. Father, you'll empower me in the name of Jesus.
47. Father all that is needful to take care of my husband and children, you will release onto me. I receive the ability and enablement to support my husband in Jesus name.

While some are still struggling to buy their first home, some parents are giving keys of homes to their children. How nice would it be if your children do not have to go through the struggles you went through. Imagine that you hand the keys to their apartment to them by the time a child is finishing from university, on the day of their graduation. Rewarding them when they have proven themselves that they are responsible and focused on excelling in life!!!! Oh, what a beautiful sight that will be!

When other children their age are still struggling, you've already set your children on a great path, that is the life I want to live, I don't want to be a liability of a mother or a wife.

Pray now and say:
48. Father I don't want to be a liability, make me a flourishing tree in my

home, one which is deeply rooted and able to withstand every financial storm or need.
49. I refuse to be shaken financially, spiritually, in the name of Jesus.
50. I receive financial enablement in the name of Jesus so that by the time my children are ready, Father I'll be giving them great inheritance.
51. Because of my godly choices, i will save my children from exposure to a life of unnecessary hardship. Lord, their path into prosperity will be easy because you will give me the ability to empower them right from the beginning in Jesus name.
52. Father, I am asking, because I am only as good as my decisions, Lord from this minute onward, every stupid decision I have made in the past, that is costing money, in the name of Jesus from tonight I ask that you help me, to correct them, Lord in the name of Jesus.
53. Father help me to stop making wrong choices and decisions that will waste the income, entitlement and inheritance of my household in the name of Jesus.
54. From tonight I receive supernatural wisdom to align my choices with God's plans, thereby achieving results according to God's plan

A lot of us have useful resources, the only reason we lack is that we keep putting them in wrong and undeserving places. Simple examples of this include when you buy every dress you see in different colours or you buy every beautiful shoes you see because you like them or even because you want to be part of every party in town. The people for whose party you bought the shoes may never even acknowledge that you attended their party. Yet, you're just wasting all your income on possessions that lose value straight after you purchased them– this is a form of money ritual.

Pray now and say:
55. Lord, every hidden way in which the devil is taking away my family's money and resources, in the name of Jesus, from tonight, I block

every such access.
56. Father help me to be sensible in the management of the funds you have committed to me, so I'll make the right choices on where my money goes, in the name of Jesus.
57. Lord, help me to tame my eyes and discipline myself from just buying unprofitable possessions in the mighty name of Jesus
58. Father please help me correct my appetite for the short term pleasures that is ruining my family resources in the name of Jesus.
59. Father please help me from every financial bondage I have put myself. I receive liberation right now, I remove myself right now from every bondage that is stopping my family from making progress financially in the mighty name of Jesus.

As I mentioned earlier, some of us will find some prayer points to be difficult to pray; especially if you're not ready to move on. Embrace the correction of the Lord whenever you are ready to move on. Ask that the Lord will help you, it is an addiction you need to deal with it.

Pray and say:
60. Father I have not handled the money you have put into my hands correctly, have mercy on me, forgive me, please release onto me again the keys of treasures of this world, in the name of Jesus.
61. Father help me to direct my resources towards the right things that I'll be able to save my inheritance for my children, that my husband will see me as a great treasure, Father I give you glory, Father thank you for hearing us, in Jesus name.

CONCLUSION:

My father and my Lord, I want to thank you because you know me, I'm not hidden from you, many times, my financial difficulties are due to wrong choices and decisions. I am asking that you will deliver me from every financial bondage caused by wrong choices.

I am asking especially oh Lord for the wisdom and the ability to say NO when I need to say NO to things that I do not need in Jesus name.

You have given us all that pertains to life of godliness, everything that our home needs to be excellent, even for our needs to be met. Father I am praying for wisdom for profitable ventures in Jesus name. I receive the ability to make money, ability to make work, in the name of Jesus.

Father, I ask that you enrich me, so I can enrich many in my generation; henceforth, as I labour, I shall have good results. You said they will be a difference between those who serve you and who don't. Father I am praying, regarding my household, because we serve you, we will not lack anything good. Our path shines brighter and brighter unto perfection in the name of Jesus.

We give you all the glory, we give you all the honour, blessed be your name oh Lord in Jesus we've prayed, Amen.

Chapter 2
FAVOUR FOR OUR CHILDREN

INTRODUCTION:

Our children need favour in life and all through life. The world is becoming more competitive looking at happenings around; our children will need supernatural favour to proceed beyond their counterparts. They need an edge to make progress and to thrive in this environment. I am trusting that the Lord will help us to connect and to lay a foundation that will last forever through the course of this prayer session. I will be sharing specific stories from the bible and also from life experiences. I hope we can benefit and pick a few things to help you through this prayer session.

Samuel 9:1-8, 13 KJV

And David said, is there yet any that is left of the house of Saul, that I may shew him kindness for Jonathan's sake? And there was of the house of Saul a servant whose name was Ziba. And when they had called him unto David, the king said unto him, Art thou Ziba? And he said, thy servant is he. And the king said, is there not yet any of the house of Saul, that I may shew the kindness of God unto him? And Ziba said unto the king, Jonathan hath yet a son, which is lame on his feet. And the king said unto him, where is he? And Ziba said unto the king, Behold, he is in the house of Machir, the son of Ammiel, in Lo-debar. Then king David sent, and fetched him out of the house of Machir, the son of Ammiel, from Lo-debar. Now when Mephibosheth, the son of Jonathan, the son of Saul, was come unto David, he fell on his face, and did reverence. And David said, Mephibosheth. And he answered, Behold thy servant! And

David said unto him, Fear not: for I will surely shew thee kindness for Jonathan thy father's sake and will restore thee all the land of Saul thy father; and thou shalt eat bread at my table continually. And he bowed himself, and said, what is thy servant, that thou shouldest look upon such a dead dog as I am? So, Mephibosheth dwelt in Jerusalem: for he did eat continually at the king's table; and was lame on both his feet.

Further reading of the story reveals exactly what happened to Mephibosheth, the bible says that Mephibosheth had been living in Lodebar - which was by no means an enviable place at all. Mephibosheth was relegated to this place, he was been forgotten, he was among the lowest of lows, but one day the king woke up and decided that it was time for him to remember Mephibosheth.

We are going to pray for our children, because many things happen in the course of their lives and we need the Lord's favour to work on their behalf. As I mentioned in one of our prayer sessions.

> "Great things do not just happen to people by chance or by luck; they are as a result some precepts established beforehand"

We are going to be laying the precepts, we are going to be laying the foundation upon which we will be build, upon which our children will build, upon which our children will prosper. Sisters, as you connect, I want you to ask God for the future of your children, for the time when you are with them and for the time when they are away from you.

Now, Pray

1. That the Lord's favour will speak for your children in the mighty name of Jesus.

As we heard in that story, Mephibosheth was forgotten, Mephibosheth was in Lodebar, can it get any worse? He was a son that was supposed to live within the royal premises, he was supposed to be within the palace, but the bible says he was lame in both feet, the fact that he was lame means that every other thing that everybody was supposed to be struggling to get, he couldn't get, but one day, David remembered him.

2. Father out of the depth of your mercy and grace, please open the book of remembrance unto my children.

Mephibosheth was in Lodebar, he was in a place where he was forgotten, he was in a place where he was relegated.

3. Father, regarding my children, I ask for their past and present entitlement be remembered and honoured.
4. I ask that the path be set now for their future entitlements to be allocated to them promptly, in the name of Jesus.

There are times when the goodness due us remains hidden until we step out of our comfort zone and go all out and get them. The bible says in:

Matthew 11:12 that
"from the time of John the Baptist the kingdom
of God suffers violence and the violent will take it by force."

5. Lord every goodness that is due my children, every goodness that is due me, wherever they have been hidden, I ask that you release your angels to go ahead and restore them.
6. In cases where this has been forcefully withheld, I ask that heaven will drag them out, in the mighty name of Jesus. I release the word of God into the hiding place and storage space of all that is due me. I command that they be released in the mighty name of Jesus.
7. Every goodness due my children, every promotion due my children and every inheritance due them, I expose such, for their benefit, in the mighty name of Jesus. I bring you to a place where my children can lay hold on you, to a place where I can lay hold on you, to a place where my husband can lay hold on you.

It happened that Ziba, a servant at the time the king was nearby when David came. Ziba was a servant, just hanging around in the palace premises when David asked the question about the household of Saul. I am Ziba, he said. I served under the king and I served in the time that Jonathan was alive, I know a bit about this family and the members that you are asking.

8. Lord I am asking that you will position them at strategic places to direct favour towards my way and towards my children in the mighty name of Jesus.
9. Father I am asking, everyone who needs to speak in my children's favour, will not withhold information on their account.
10. I place my children in the right place at the right time. I place myself in the right position; everybody who needs to help me will know my name, remember my name, they will know my location, they will know my description.
11. The good that is due me will not be wrongfully allocated to another due to inadequate information and advertisement.
12. Father for me, my children and my husband to be able to lay hold on that which you have planned for us, I am asking that you will

position our helpers in strategic parts of our journey, in the mighty name of Jesus.
13. We decree promptness of remembrance so that we will not miss our allocated time of restoration in the name of Jesus.

I came across a story a few years ago. There were two professors in the same university. One of them was in the Faculty of Arts, the other in the Faculty of Science. These two professors had the same surname but and first name but different middle names. The science professor was exceptional, his works were famous abroad, and he was well known. Before long, he came to the attention of a university in the United States. The university decided that they were going to honour this man for the remarkable job he was doing, and for the ongoing research work and they invited him over to receive the honours. They sent a letter of invitation for his visa from embassy, the letter contained the details of the honour to be presented to him in the USA. They also detailed that they were going to foot the bill for his flight and other things needed. This letter was mistakenly delivered to the other professor who decided to make the letter his. He took the documents, cashed the money and bought the ticket. On arrival in the United States, they received him. Everyone was excited to meet him. During his presentation, he dabbled and dabbled around. They clapped and everybody said he was talking amazing things, they assumed he had a fresh insight which they were yet to understand.

He enjoyed the rest of the stay and then he returned home. Several months later that they sent another correspondence. It stated how it was lovely to have had him in the United States, and that they were grateful to be associated with him. It was only at this point, that this man realised what had happened. He called and they said sorry we have already received this professor. This man missed his time, he missed his visitation because the description fitted that of somebody else. You are going to pray for your children.

14. Lord, demarcate my children from the crowd, make it easy for them to be located for outstanding recognition.
15. Father the good destined for my children, the good you have planned and prepared for my children will not be usurped by another, in the name of Jesus.

Peradventure ziba was not available that day, how would they have found Mephibosheth?

16. Lord, as you position people in strategic places to locate me and my children, father there shall be no confusion. My good shall not be given to another, that which is befitting to me, that which you have planned and prepared for me, that which you have planned and prepared for my children will not be mistaken in the mighty name of Jesus.
17. Another will not take the place of my children in the place you have prepared for them in destiny in the mighty name of Jesus.
18. I decree and I declare that the good you have allocated, and you have assigned to my children, they will walk into them in a timely manner in the mighty name of Jesus.

As I continued reading the story, it occurred to me that Mephibosheth received all that belonged to Jonathan, even though they were rightfully Jonathan's; properties were handed over to Mephibosheth even though he was lame.

19. Lord, no matter my children's situation now, no matter my circumstances now, I am asking oh Lord, nothing shall serve as a deterrent to those who want to help us, in the mighty name of Jesus. My children's current situation, their current placement, their current location shall not serve as a deterrent to those who want to help them in the mighty name of Jesus.
20. Father, wherever they must search, however they want to search,

father for them to locate my children, you shall give their benefactors no rest until that which is due my children has offered to them.
21. There is a way that people who are searching will give up and turn back, when they have searched and the search is not yielding quick answers. Lord, with ease, they that seek to do my children good will find and honour them. With ease they shall locate them, with ease they shall be given access to them, in the mighty name of Jesus.
22. Those who seek to do my children favour shall not be confused, regarding their identity, in Jesus name.

Esther 6:1-3 KJV
On that night could not the king sleep, and he commanded to bring the book of records of the chronicles; and they were read before the king. And it was found written, that Mordecai had told of Bigthana and Teresh, two of the king's chamberlains, the keepers of the door, who sought to lay hand on the king Ahasuerus. And the king said, what honour and dignity hath been done to Mordecai for this? Then said the king's servants that ministered unto him, there is nothing done for him.

I tell you that people will sometimes lose their sleep because of the favour they need to do to you as a result of your prayers. The bible says that the king had the official royal records brought in and his young male servant read them to the king. They discovered the report about Mordecai informing on Bigthana and Teresh, these were the two royal eunuchs among the guards protecting the king's doorway who secretly planned to kill King Ahaseur. *"What was done to honour and reward Mordecai for this"* the king asked. His young servant replied, *"nothing was done for him sir".*

You are going to pray:

23. Lord, put an urgency in the heart of every man or woman on whose hands my children's favour lie, put an urgency within their heart to act promptly in their favour.

24. Father I am asking, as the heart of kings are in your hands and as the rivers of water you turn it the way you will. Peradventure there is a man or a woman in whose hands the favour of my children lie, I ask oh Lord that sleep be taken away from their eyes until they are able to do the favour due my children.

I discovered something in Isaiah

> **Isaiah 60:2, 10-11, 14-16 KJV**
> For, behold, the darkness shall cover the earth, and gross darkness the people: but the Lord shall arise upon thee, and his glory shall be seen upon thee. And the sons of strangers shall build up thy walls, and their kings shall minister unto thee: for in my wrath I smote thee, but in my favour have I had mercy on thee. Therefore, thy gates shall be open continually; they shall not be shut day nor night; that men may bring unto thee the forces of the Gentiles, and that their kings may be brought. The sons also of them that afflicted thee shall come bending unto thee; and all they that despised thee shall bow themselves down at the soles of thy feet; and they shall call thee, The city of the Lord, The Zion of the Holy One of Israel. Whereas thou hast been forsaken and hated, so that no man went through thee, I will make thee an eternal excellency, a joy of many generations. Thou shalt also suck the milk of the Gentiles, and shalt suck the breast of kings: and thou shalt know that I the Lord am thy Saviour and thy Redeemer, the mighty One of Israel.

The nations of the world are crying wolf; however, some people are still making it even when other a struggling. They are making money through righteous means; they have not committed any sin and they are prospering despite how hard the times are.

You are going to make this declaration regarding your children

25. It does not matter how gloomy the world is, it does not matter how gloomy the countries are, it does not matter how bad the situation is, father your peculiar favour will rest upon my children, in the mighty name of Jesus.
26. The bible says when there is a pulling down and tearing down, we will say there is a lifting up. Father I decree concerning my children, in their generation oh Lord, when people are saying things are hard, when people are saying things are difficult, my children will be thriving, my children will be getting stronger and more prosperous through righteous means in the mighty name of Jesus.
27. They will not dupe anyone; they will not cheat but the blessing of God will single them out and they will prosper in every way in all that they lay their hands upon in the mighty name of Jesus.
28. In as much as the world is crying of difficulty, my children will bloom in the name of Jesus, because the Lord will shine upon them my children you will bloom like a cedar in Lebanon in the Mighty name of Jesus.
29. My children, you will bring forth your fruits in due season.
30. You shall not be delayed because the world is delayed, you shall not be delayed because the economy is delayed in the mighty name of Jesus.
31. Everything you deserve in the mighty name of Jesus, you will lay your hands upon them in the right season in a timely fashion, in a timely order in the mighty name of Jesus.
32. Lord, you will bless the sweat and the effort of my children, the favour of the lord will make them blessed, the favour of the lord will make them exemplified, they shall be singled out in favour in the mighty name of Jesus.

33. When doors of favour are being shut against people, my children will thrive, when doors of favour are being shut, when they are saying they are no longer accepting people in great places, my children, as an exception, you will be favoured, in the mighty name of Jesus.
34. My children, the door will be flung wide open for you to receive welcome into greatness where others are being turned down.
35. The law which limits others will not limit you when the time of favour shall come for you in the mighty name of Jesus. The door that is limiting people and barring them from making progress in the mighty Name of Jesus I say it will fling wide open, wide and open for you to be allowed access in the mighty name of Jesus.
36. I pray that the favour of the lord will give you increase beyond your natural effort. The favour God which makes you to have a huge result despite the little work shall continue increase you.
37. My children, I decree favour upon you beyond understandable reasons in the name of Jesus. When people cannot understand, I say the favour of the Lord shall open doors for you in the mighty name of Jesus. Little effort will bring great success because the favour of the Lord is upon your sweat, In Jesus name we have prayed.

> **2Kings 13:23 NIV**
> But the Lord was gracious to them and had compassion and showed concern for them because of his covenant with Abraham, Isaac and Jacob. To this day he has been unwilling to destroy them or banish them from his presence.

Our children sometimes walk away from the path we lead them, our children walk away from where we have asked them to go but you know what, there is a covenant that the lord holds with a woman, there is a covenant the Lord holds with a mother, that covenant transcends even the sin the children commit, the mercy of the Lord covers them, the favour of the Lord isolates them for what would been a judgment on them. The bible gave an example of that covenant in the scriptures above.

You are going to pray now:

38. Father, because of my cry, my children will experience favour all through their lives in the mighty name of Jesus, even when they miss it and they deserve judgement and punishment, father the covenant I have with you in this time of prayer tonight, will stand and will shield my children from punishment, it will shield them for judgement in the mighty name of Jesus.
39. Because you have a covenant with me, a covenant of mercy towards my children, father you will not destroy them, neither will you cast them away from your presence, in the mighty name of Jesus.
40. My children will experience favour from you Lord, they will experience mercy by reason of this prayer in the mighty name of Jesus. Even when they miss it, father your mercy will bring them back to you instead of destroying them in your anger, father your mercy will reinstate them in the mighty name of Jesus.

The bible says I will have mercy on whom I will have mercy and I will compassion on whom I will have compassion, that means the lord chooses and he decides who he wants to have mercy on, who he wants to forgive, who he wants to have compassion on. Romans 9:15.

41. Lord I ask that your mercy and compassion will meet my children in the mighty name of Jesus, in the time of trouble, when they miss it oh Lord, your mercy and compassion will meet them by the reason of this prayer they will not face judgement, they will not face punishment even when they deserve it, your mercy will speak for them, your favour will overshadow judgment in the mighty name of

Jesus. I am pleading Lord on behalf of my children from now and for the future in the name of Jesus.

42. Peradventure they miss it, peradventure they walk away, peradventure they stumble, father, mercy will speak for them by the reason of this prayer Lord, by the reason of this prayer Lord, mercy will speak for them in their future, even in their current stage in the name of Jesus.

> **Proverbs 16:7,13,15 (NIV)**
> When the Lord takes pleasure in anyone's way, he causes their enemies to make peace with them. Kings take pleasure in honest lips; they value the one who speaks what is right. When a king's face brightens, it means life; his favour is like a rain cloud in spring.

The scriptures explain that when the king decides to turn his gaze towards you, life becomes your portion. Whether or not you were destined to die and be destroyed, it will not matter anymore.

This is what I want you to pray:

43. Say father, turn your face towards my children, behold them with the full glare of your favour. Father turn your face towards my children, let them experience favour as you look upon them, let my children experience favour as you look upon them. The bible says there is life in the light of your face, my children cannot face calamity when the lord is looking upon them, they cannot run into trouble when the lord is looking upon them.

44. Say lord look upon my children with the full glare of your favour, with the full glare of your faith from this day onwards in the mighty name of Jesus. Father I pray and I ask that you Look upon my children, look upon my household, look upon me, look upon my husband with the full glare of your face oh Lord. In the name of Jesus.

The bible says his favour is like a cloud that brings the springs rain. Do you know what happens during spring? Flowers come forth, trees come back to life, everything receives life, when the lord sends rain. *(Proverbs 16:5)*

45. Lord, like the cloud that brings the rain of spring, let your favour rest upon my children in the mighty name of Jesus.
46. Lord, regarding my children, their ways will be pleasing unto you - favour automatically comes upon their path when their ways are pleasing.
47. In the name of Jesus, my son will not turn his back against you, my daughter will not turn her back against you, their ways will be pleasing unto you so that favour will be their portion in the mighty name of Jesus, I decree and declare Lord in the name of Jesus.

There is something about favour that breaks protocols; I have experienced this so many times. When you are denied access because you are judged wrongly as not qualified; but things turn around as you turn back and have a word with the lord. Even though they usually do not do this, they do it for you. Something that happened to me a few years ago, I also shared it on *Thypreciousjewels* platforms at that time. I was working in this department where there were not many people my colour; it was extremely busy and on one of the days I was not able to purchase my usual sandwich as they'd ran out; the queue was long behind me and everybody wanted their. I looked back and decided that I wasn't going to settle for what I do not like. I couldn't accept anything else. So, I informed the lady at the till the sand which I desired. The lady looked at me and she said they'd run out. I quietly adviced her that it was what I wanted to which she replied that she was the only one serving, but she left the till, and went to make that sandwich for me while everybody waited, that is favour.

You may say, oh, it is just sandwich, how about if it was an admission. How about if you needed to be admitted into a plane and the doors were already shut? I have been there before too.

How about if you needed to be admitted into a university and they say they already have enough people how about if you needed to get into a place?

How about if it was an office and they say that the application has already closed?

There are deadlines everywhere. There ard gates everywhere, restricting access to greatness. We don't just accept a No! As long as we know what has been freely given to us by God, we push through the doors until they open.

48. *Lord, I do not care how it happens, I am asking for favour which breaks natural protocols for my children in the name of Jesus.*
49. *There are some doors so secure, only the supernatural favour of God can open them. It is this kind of favour I am decreeing for my children in the mighty name of Jesus. From today onward, I am decreeing lord, favour which is exemplary upon my children in the name of Jesus. Favour that will stand out upon my children in the name of Jesus, that doors will be opened unto them on their own accord in the mighty name of Jesus, father they will not even need to ask, they will not even need to beg, doors will open upon my children, doors of favour in the name of Jesus, upon my husband, upon myself in the name of Jesus.*

The bible says in Daniel 1:5, 8-11, 13

Daniel made up his mind that he was not going to allow himself to eat the food meant for the gods, he decided that he was going to approach the people in authority, he spoke to the first person in charge, the first person said, couldn't help him; he was afraid he might get in to trouble and they may be killed, he said but, go ahead and Daniel took it a step further, he went to the next person in authority and he spoke to the person, he says you know this thing I am dealing with is quite serious, I need an issue to be sorted out. And the issue that need to be sorted out is that my children need to be in the right place. Some of your children might be denied university admission because they did not meet the cut-off mark, you are not begging you are not pleading, you are not bribing anybody, you will say my children have the required mark and they deserve to be hear and because of that, the favour of the lord will go and speak for you. They might say your children will not fall within the area we want to accept, you will say I am sorry, my children are from Zion and because of this, this is their inheritance and they will take it. My dear sisters, Daniel said I agree with you that they may kill you but that is not my business now. My business is that my children will prosper, in that I will obey the king and I will not defile my hands and I will get this result I desire and because of this.

50. *Stand in the gap for your children for whether you are there or not, the door of favour will not shut against them in the mighty name of Jesus.*
51. *Decree and declare, whatever nation of the world and whatever the platform, the door of favour will never shut against your children in the mighty name of Jesus.*

The bible says, Daniel went to the guard who had been placed in charge of them and says compare us with the young men who are eating food from the royal court based on the decision on how we look.

You are going to pray, say:
52. *Father Lord, for every law of the land that will put my children in distress as they obey you, I ask for supernatural exemption. Father, exempt my children as they take a stand in righteousness. You will back them up with favour that they cannot explain in the name of Jesus. As my children move towards the direction and the path that you have set for them, you will back them up in favour in the name of Jesus.*
53. *I decree, supernatural exemption in the name of Jesus, from every law that limits in the name of Jesus. I say the favour of the lord will make them exempt from every law that limits them in the mighty name of Jesus.*
54. *The favour of the lord will make them exempt from every law that will harm them, the favour of the lord will make them exempt from every law that will stop or limit life results.*

The Lord favoured Daniel on multiple levels, you are going to pray,
55. *Every door my children will knock seeking that which you have prepared for them, will open on all levels. In the mighty name of Jesus.*

56. They will not be approved at lower level but refused at national level. whatever the lord does is perfect, whatever the lord does there is no fault in it. My children I decree, for every level you are favoured, at the lowest level you are favoured, at the medium level you are favoured, at the final level you are favoured in the mighty name of Jesus.
57. I decree, my children, nobody will hinder you, nobody will be able to stop you. Nobody will ban you from going ahead to that level that the lord has planned in the name of Jesus.

CONCLUSION

Our father and our God we want to thank you for your favour that speaks on behalf of our children. Father, I am standing in agreement with my sisters and my brothers who are joining in this prayers and I am asking oh Lord, as many of us as have been forgotten and our rightful places have been taken over by others, father we begin to ask tonight that the favour of the Lord will search and will find out that which is befitting and is due us in the name of Jesus. Father we specifically ask that as many children as have their inheritances locked away in the hidden places that have been usurped by another, father we remove those who are sitting upon those seats, we remove them forcefully in the name of Jesus.

We say everything that belongs to us, every good that belongs to my children, every good that belongs to my children, every good that belongs to me that was taken over by another, we unsettled them and we say be thou removed in the mighty name of Jesus. And father, we decree and declare in the mighty name of Jesus that which belongs to us, we take over in the name of Jesus, father we ask there shall be no confusion, there shall be no confusion oh lord. When the time you set to favour Zion comes, that time is the time, there shall be no confusion lord, there shall be no delay.

Father Lord God almighty, we ask oh lord for swift recognition, for right placement, for divine and strategic positioning in the name of Jesus for our children. We ask Lord God almighty, as you granted Daniel favour at every level, we receive favour at every level in the name of Jesus, we will not just go through the little levels and the senior ones will be become a difficulty, father we receive easy passage, easy access in the name of Jesus. The favour of the Lord will overwhelm us, I am asking that you will glare your *full face upon our children, and you will favour them.*

We give you glory and honour, father thank you lord, because upon this mountain, upon this altar, there shall be testimonies of your goodness towards our children, we speak favour in the morning of their lives, we speak favour in the noon of their lives, we speak favour in the night time of their lives, we give you glory oh Lord, thank you because you have heard us for in Jesus name we have prayed. Amen.

Chapter 3
PEACE FOR MY CHILDREN

INTRODUCTION

The bible says in:

> *Isaiah 54:13,*
>
> *'All your children shall be taught of the Lord and great shall be the peace of your children.'*

That means a child that is taught of the Lord is the one entitled to peace. So, we need to teach our children of about the Lord because they will not get these lessons or teaching anywhere else. You are going to be praying for yourself and for your children; you are going to be asking that the Lord will enable and help you stand in the gap and pray regarding your children, in the mighty name of Jesus.

Firstly, you are going to be praying for yourselves; ask that the Lord will help you:

Prayer points:

1. Lord, peradventure there is anything in me the enemy may want to present as an excuse to take advantage of my children, Father, please purge me of such in the mighty name of Jesus.

We may have put our hands many times into things that are ungodly. The Lord has asked specifically that we pray regarding this.

2. Lord, if there is anything the enemy will hold on to, anything he will use to oppress my children and take their peace away through me, let your mercy speak on my behalf right now.

3. Father I am asking that you will purge me right now, please cleanse me by your mighty power, peradventure there is a seed of corruption in me the enemy will want to lay hold on or to use against me or use to take away the peace of my children. Father I am asking

in the name of Jesus.

4. *Father I am asking that your mercy will speak for me, even in the area I am deficient and I am not aware, Father I ask in the name of Jesus that you will open the eyes of my understanding that I may know, that I may see clearly as you want me to, in the mighty name of Jesus.*
5. *Father I ask oh Lord God Almighty, that you will investigate my past, look review my present and let your mercy erase every seed I have sown that will yield unease, trouble or distress for my children.*
6. *Father I relinquish myself of every consequences and repercussions scheduled to send my children into oppression and bondage in the mighty name of Jesus.*

I will share a scenario the Lord brought to attention; during my youthful years in the university and early years of work, many young men promise marriage sisters. These young men will for instance ask the sisters to sleep with them that they will to marry them, they promise heaven and earth and they will make promises in order to make them commit to a relationship. At the end of it all, they leave that sister and marry someone else. A situation like this is a foundation that will take the mercy of the Lord to save you from.

Making promises and going into commitments like these and afterwards leaving the sister to marry another is dangerous; when you settle with children, family also seems as though everything is going on well. There is something about the law of the seed and harvest: it will catch up at some point. If it doesn't catch up with you, it catches up with your children. Children sometimes go through hard times as a result of the seed their parents sowed. The Lord wants you to stand in the gap right now and pray. Lord and we are asking that:

7. In the name of Jesus, peradventure there is a seed I have sown that will bring turmoil, that would bring torture, that will take away the peace of my children in the future, Lord, I ask that your mercy will relieve me of the consequences of every mistake I have made; your mercy will relieve me of every commitment I have made that I am entitled to suffer punishment for; my children will not suffer punishment as a result of my action, in the mighty name of Jesus.

8. Father, this is my prayer today oh God, let your mercy speak for me, let your mercy speak for my children, let your mercy speak oh Lord, in the mighty name of Jesus.

We have shared stories on THYPRECIOUSJEWELS on why marriage is a good thing. But we also know that there are many things happening in the world, things fighting against the home. The home is being attacked from every side. People are finding reasons why they should not commit to marriage. You are going to ask:

9. Lord, enable me and give me the wisdom to make my marriage a beautiful place for my children to grow in, to make my marriage one that my children will be able to have peace within the home.

There can never be peace in a home where husband and wife are constantly arguing, and the husband slaps his wife about. The children do not experience peace and they will have no understanding of what peace is.

10. Father, I receive for myself today, wisdom to live with my husband in

a peaceful home environment, wisdom to raise my children in a peaceful home environment, wisdom to stand aright and do the right thing, wisdom to speak a word in season, in the name of Jesus.

11. *I receive wisdom to teach my children how to live in a marriage relationship, Father I receive in the mighty name of Jesus, whatever they need to learn from you to make their home a peaceful one, Father you will give unto me Lord, in the mighty name of Jesus.*

12. *It is crucial to learn the right things. Lord, I will not teach my children the wrong way of marriage; I will not teach them the wrong lifestyle of marriage, in the mighty name of Jesus.*

I have discovered that whether our children say it or not, they are watching us. These children are looking at the way we speak to our husbands, they are looking at the way the husband speaks to you. If your husband decides to slap you, your child will have it registered as the right thing to do.

You are going to pray now, and say:

13. *Devil, in the name of Jesus, I command you to take your hands off my home. I will raise my children in a godly environment and great shall be their peace, in the mighty name of Jesus.*

14. *Father, I declare regarding my home; my home belongs to You. I receive the wisdom to live with my husband, the wisdom to have a profitable marriage.*

15. *I receive the wisdom to make my marriage to profit me emotionally, psychologically, monetarily, spiritually and health-wise.*

16. *Father, Lord, I receive your wisdom right now to live, in every aspect you have designed for me to enjoy my home, in the name of Jesus.*

and in the name of Jesus.

17. Satan, I command you to take your hands of my home; I command you to take your hands of my property, and my marriage. I decree that my marriage is a peaceful place for my children to grow, my marriage is a peaceful place for my children to thrive, in the mighty name of Jesus.

18. Every force of separation, every force of division that may be at work in my home right now, I command you to be removed, in the mighty name of Jesus. Every force of division the enemy may want to put in a place to destroy my children, I cancel you. I say, I come against division in my home, I come against separation in my home, I come against turmoil and torture in my home, in the mighty name of Jesus.

19. I decree that my home is a peaceful place for my children to grow in. I decree it is a peaceful place for my children to thrive in, in the mighty name of Jesus. My children will find my home a peaceful place, a place of joy, a place where they can speak up, a place where they can be fed and be nourished.

20. My children shall not see my home as a place of torture, in the mighty name of Jesus. Father I give you free hand to operate in my home, I give you free hand to do it the way you want; I give you free hand to correct me, I give you free hand to correct my husband, I give you free hand to make our home what you created it to be, that we would raise great children from my family, in the mighty name of Jesus.

The Bible says in:
> **Proverbs 29:15.**
> *"CORRECT YOUR CHILDREN AND THEY WILL BE WISE".*
> *Children who are out of control disgrace their mothers.*

21. Lord, the wisdom to correct my children when I need to correct them, I receive in the mighty name of Jesus.
22. The wisdom to tell them off when I need to tell them off, the wisdom to point them in the right direction for them to go, Father, I receive that wisdom for them in the mighty name of Jesus. My children will not be unruly, unbridled children, they will be corrected, and they will be trained in the way of the Lord, they will be loved, and will be corrected in a loving manner.
23. In the name of Jesus. I will not destroy them by reason of correction. I will not knock down their confidence by reason of correction. I will correct them positively; I will correct them in a way that their lives shall be transformed; I will correct them in a way that will take them to great places in life in the mighty name of Jesus.
24. Father, your Word says that children who are out of control disgrace their parents. My children will not bring disgrace to me because I will correct them in the way they need to go in the name of Jesus.

Every child needs to have firm understanding of what is wrong and right.

25. Lord, help me to teach my children and show them what is right and what is wrong.
26. Every child needs to be led, every child needs to be directed, every child needs to be instructed. HELP ME LORD.

Some of us do not understand what is right or wrong, therefore unable to train their children aright.

Say:

27. Father, help me to correct my children the right way, help me to teach them the right way to go, help me to instruct them the right way to go, in the name of Jesus.'
28. Lord, teach me by yourself that I will be able to teach my children the right way to go, in the mighty name of Jesus. Father teach me, instruct my heart, instruct my spirit, instruct me that I may know what to do in the name of Jesus. I will not show my children the wrong direction, I will not show them the wrong attitude, I will not give them the wrong emphasis in life oh Lord, in the mighty name of Jesus.

Many of us are busy; we are very busy taking care of our family responsibilities. Some of us working many hours and shifts that we forget to create time to the most important project we have on our hands - *OUR CHILDREN*.

29. You are going to ask that the Lord will help you, that your time will be allocated appropriately to training your children in the mighty name of Jesus.
30. Every ungainful employment, every ungainful relationship, every relationship and commitment that takes me away from my children and does not allow me to teach them and train them in the way that the Lord has designed to prosper them in life, I ask Lord, relieve me of such, in the name of Jesus.
31. Lord you will help me to do away with unimportant people, irrelevant and unimportant associations in my life, in the name of Jesus.
32. Every association, everything, every person occupying my time and

taking away the precious time I should be sowing into my children's destiny, Lord, please take them away from me, in the name of Jesus.
33. Lord I enter into a covenant of responsibility with you, over my children. From today, I will begin to sow profitable time into my children's future in the name of Jesus.

We are on assignment, because we have never raised these children before; we are new to this project. You are going to ask that the Lord will help you. When you are taking part in something you have never done before, you need to know how to do it well, especially when you only have one opportunity to raise the children.

34. You are going ask that the Lord will enable you, you are going to ask that the Lord will sustain you, and you are going to ask that the Lord will help you in the name of Jesus. You will ask that all that you need will be released and be supplied unto you, in the name of Jesus.
35. Father, I have just one shot at this, I am only going to be a mother to these children once in my lifetime. Therefore, Lord, I ask that you enable and equip me; that which you have equipped me with, help me Lord, to use them appropriately, in the mighty name of Jesus. I will raise them the way you want me to raise them; I have just one opportunity oh Lord. I ask for you to help me, that my children will be raised appropriately. I will not mess up on this task, in the name of Jesus.
36. Father, I will do it right and I will get it right, in the name of Jesus. Father Lord God Almighty, at the first attempt and the first shot, I will get it, in Jesus name we have prayed.

Some of had traumatic childhood; some of us went through so many hardships that makes it difficult to train our children without taking out our experiences on them. The way some of us talk to our children is borne out of our experience. Some people were molested, some were traumatized from childhood; they now find it difficult to connect their children because of that.

37. You are going to ask now that the Lord will heal you, that you will not transfer aggression to these children in the mighty name of Jesus.

Some of us find it difficult to love our children the right way because we have experience failure in relationships. We look at them and we see the men who have hurt us, the men who have messed us up.

You are going to ask the Lord to:
38. Help me, Lord; let my focus be on my children and let it be right. Father, I receive the right spirit, right mind, and right disposition towards them, in the name of Jesus.
39. Lord, my children will flourish under my care, they will flourish under my eyes; I will not miss it, I will not get it wrong, in the mighty name of Jesus.
40. Every hurt in my heart that will not allow me to be the best parent to my children, Lord, you will heal, in the name of Jesus.
41. Every trauma or abuse in my childhood preventing me from loving my children, Father, heal me. You will heal me, in the mighty name of Jesus.

Children often ask questions; a lot of them do not even know where to go. **We are going to pray now that:**
42. The Lord will put the right words in my mouth for my children.

Children come home sometimes not desiring to talk to us; some just want to be quiet. **We shall pray now and ask:**
43. Lord, give me insight that I will see what my children are going through, that I will know what to say to them. I will know how to question and address them, in the name of Jesus.

Those with teenage children know how they can be; it is almost impossible to talk to them when they don't want to talk to you.

Pray now and say:
44. Father give me insight into what my children are going through. Lord give me insight, open my eyes that I may see and understand what my children are going through, in the mighty name of Jesus.
45. Father give me insight regarding my children's lives that I will know how to take care of my children, that I will know how to address them when they are challenged, scared, threatened or have been chastised externally.
46. Father Lord God almighty, I receive insight to know what is happening to my children per time, and how to address them. I will know how to correct them and support them; Father in this child-rearing business, guide me, in Jesus name.

Once again, we are going to pray, when there is peace within their body of a child, that child is at peace through and through .Some children do not have peace within their body. Children with medical conditions and those unwell in any way, have no peace.

You are going to pray now, and you are going to decree peace in your children's body; say:
47. Father, I speak unto my children's body, and I decree peace within their bodies in the name of Jesus.
48. Father, I receive peace for my children's body; the enemy will not torment their bodies in the mighty name of Jesus.
49. My children's body will not be afflicted or tormented with disease or illness. I decree peace in my children's body, my children will dwell in peace; there shall be peace within their bodies, in Jesus name.
50. I decree that every part of my children's body shall prosper, every part of their body shall flourish and be preserved, in the name of Jesus. There shall be none insufficient nor any that is overactive in the name of Jesus.

51.   I decree that in every part of my children's body, my sons, my daughters, there is peace. Your bodily functions are perfect condition, in the mighty name of Jesus.
52.   My children's bodies shall not lack anything good. They shall not suffer for anything called deficiency. I decree now that whatever my children's bodies need to function properly is released unto them, in the name of Jesus. There shall be peace within their bodies, and they will not lack anything good, in Jesus name.

You are going to pray for peace in your children's mind.
53.   Decree that there is peace in their mind.

Some things going on in the of children are sometimes unbelievable; some of our teenagers don't even know that they are hearing different things. Some of them are hearing that it is ok for them to sleep with around, some are hearing other things; they do not know, they are confused.

Decree now:
54.   Father, in the name of Jesus, my children's mind is sound.
55.   Their minds shall not be contaminated by friends and acquaintances in Jesus name.
56.   Lord, you will preserve my children from every contamination, and they shall be preserved, in the name of Jesus.

I decree, Lord, that:
57.   Their mind is preserved
58.   Their thoughts are preserved
59.   Their choices are preserved.
60.   Their reasoning shall be fruitful.
61.   They have the right perception about their future
62.   They have a right perception about God.
63.   They have a right perception about life
64.   They have a right and godly perception about me and my role in

their lives.
65. They have a right perception about scripture in the mighty name of Jesus.

You will now pray for peace in your children's spirit. A spirit that is distressed cannot function properly. When the spirit is stressed, the body cannot work properly.

Therefore, we shall pray:
66. *Father I ask today, that you take over my children's spirit, they shall not be inhabited by any false spirit. They shall not be inhabited by any evil spirit, in the Name of Jesus.*
67. *Lord, preserve my children's spirit from contamination, in the name of Jesus.*

Psalms 29:11
The Lord will strength unto his people.

Peace is a blessing from the Lord. So many people that have money and can afford anything they want but there is no peace of minds.

68. *Lord bless my children with peace all round about.*
69. *There will be peace for them in the morning, afternoon and at night.*
70. *There will be peace when they are at home; there will be peace when they go out and there will be peace in every aspect of their lives, in the mighty name of Jesus.*
71. *There shall be peace for my children: they shall not be troubled, neither shall they be sorrowful. Father I decree this concerning my children in Jesus name.*

Psalms 119:165
Great peace have they which love thy law; nothing shall offend them.

72. My children you shall love the law of the Lord; that is the certificate that they present before they get peace. My sons and daughters will love Your law, oh Lord and it will delight You, in the mighty name of Jesus.
73. Your law, oh Lord will be their daily focus. They will not listen to the voice of strangers and they will not be deceived into unholy living, in the name of Jesus.
74. I decree that he law of the lord will be my children's sustenance and meditation. My sons and daughters will love the Lord the morning, in the afternoon and at night, in the name of Jesus.
75. I decree over you, my children, as you love the Lord, He will preserve you with His peace. As you love the Lord, you shall not stumble. This is His plan and purpose for you: you will meditate on it day and night, in the mighty name of Jesus. In Jesus name.

Isaiah 54:10
For the mountains shall depart, and the hills be removed; but my kindness shall not depart from thee, neither shall the covenant of my peace be.

You are going to stand in agreement with the Lord. God says that no matter what is happening in the world around us, nothing will touch the covenant of peace he has with our children, nothing will touch it.

Let us pray:
76. Lord whatever is happening in the world anywhere, be it calamity or disaster, Father Lord God Almighty, your covenant of peace with my children will stand, in the name of Jesus.
77. When people are being destroyed and nations are being thrown amiss and asunder, Father, your covenant of peace with my children will be reinstated; your covenant of peace with my children will be guarded, in the name of Jesus.

78. My children will not experience turmoil like the world around them experiences. They will be preserved, oh Lord, from calamity and shall stand solid, in the mighty name of Jesus.
79. No matter what is happening around them, when the world is saying there is a casting down, my children will be recording testimonies of lifting, in the name of Jesus.
80. When the whole world is being confused and thrown into confusion, my children will stand steady and strong, in the name of Jesus. Peace shall surround them; peace shall be their portion and they will stand in righteousness, in the name of Jesus.
81. Father, even in their school, when there is commotion and there is confusion, my children will stand strong in peace, in the name of Jesus. They shall not be destroyed in the name of Jesus. Father we thank you, for in Jesus name.

Isaiah 55:12
You will go out in joy and be led forth in peace; the mountains and hills will burst into song before you, and all the trees of the field will clap.

You bring solution to the world when the mountain that are supposed to stand in your way burst out in clapping because of your presence. What is supposed to sound as a hindrance to others is already celebrating you before you arrive; that is what happens when the peace of the Lord is your portion. The bible says *you will be led forth with peace*. It did not say you will be led forth because you are strong, it says *you will be led forth with peace*.

82. I decree regarding you my sons and daughters, you will go out in Joy, and you will be led forth in peace in the name of Jesus.
83. What is supposed to destroy others will not destroy you, because the peace of the Lord will go before you, in the name of Jesus.

CONCLUSION

Our Father and our God, we thank you for today, we thank you, Lord God Almighty, as you will lead us not to relent in this prayer, because there are people you have planned to restore today so that they can start to train their children the way you want them to train them.

Father, as many as are within this group, I ask, oh Lord, that you will not give them a burden that is beyond them, in the name of Jesus. I ask for any woman who has been hurt and wounded and because of this, finds it difficult to raise children according to your standard; Father, I ask that you will heal them, and you will restore them in the mighty name of Jesus.

Father, we agree in the name of Jesus, that for every man and or woman connected to this prayer, peace will start to be their portion from today in Jesus name. I pray regarding our children oh Lord, I say peace shall be their portion. They shall have peace within their mind, they shall have peace within their bodies, they shall have peace within their spirit, in the mighty name of Jesus.

Father you said they shall go forth with joy; I agree that my children shall go forth with joy, in the name of Jesus; I agree that my children shall be led forth with peace. I decree, Lord, that as they are led forth with peace, mountains shall clap at their sight. For every difficulty and challenges people would face that makes life difficult for them, there shall be a breakthrough like never at the approach of my children, in the mighty name of Jesus.

I glorify you because you have heard me; Father, I pray specially for my everyone connected, and I ask for the wisdom to make their homes a pleasant and peaceful place for their children to grow. I say Father Lord, they have wisdom to know how to do it, that their children will find peace in the *homes where they are raised. I thank you for the wisdom to live and relate with our spouses, even the difficult ones, in the mighty name of Jesus.*

We bless your holy name because you have always heard us. We exalt you Lord; thank you for this time of prayer. Blessed be your name, oh Lord, in Jesus name we have prayed.

Amen

Chapter 4
LOCATION

INTRODUCTION

In this chapter, we shall pray about the location of our children. These are the prayer points the Lord would have us dwell on and I trust God that he will help us to pray right in the name of Jesus.

Location is very important. I mean, we are wherever we are because at a point in time, we decided that we were going to move to that area. And it is amazing that whatever happens to you in life, most of the time, it is as a result of where you are and as a result of where you have found yourself. There are a few stories that I'll like to share with us detailing what happens to people when they are in the wrong place or when they find themselves in wrong situations.

We have used Jacob as a prayer point quite a few times, asking that the Lord will direct our steps just as the Lord directed the steps of Jacob, even to find the future wife. But I realized something: The Bible says in:

> *Genesis 33:18-20*
>
> *After he left Paddan-Aram, Jacob came safely to the city of Shechem in the land of Canaan and he camped near the city. Then he purchased a portion of land from the sons of Hammond, Shechem's father for a hundred pieces of money; there he pitched his tent, set up an altar and called it "The God of Israel is God".*

This gentleman called Jacob, bought a piece of land and named that piece of Land in the name of the Lord. Essentially, you would have expected that once somebody named something in the name of the Lord, that it will succeed. No! That was not the case. It doesn't automatically succeed because they named it in the name of the Lord. Sometimes, we drag people into our business, we also drag God into it, and we say the Lord has asked us to do them or saying it is the Lord who gave use wisdom to do this. But is it the Lord?

Is it the Lord who has led you and is he going to lead your children into situations and circumstances where they will find themselves in life? The Bible says that *Diana, the daughter whom Leah had born to Jacob went out to meet the women of that country in which her father had settled.* The story continues to explain how Diana was sexually violated in that land. The Bible says *that his sons were aggrieved, and they said, 'No, we can't allow this...'* But I ask, who was it that brought this on? Who caused the problem? The problem was caused by Jacob because he settled in the wrong place.

Now Pray:
1. *Lord, I pray for my children, and I ask that in the mighty name of Jesus, that you will quicken my steps away from every location I will settle, every location where I will take my break in life, that will put my children or myself in a position of calamity and disgrace.*
2. *Oh Lord God Almighty, please hasten my steps away from every such place of I have chosen or that may be ahead of me that will cause my children to experience disgrace, in the mighty name of Jesus.*
3. *Father I ask in the mighty name of Jesus that you will quicken the steps of my children away from destruction. Quicken their steps away from violation, away from that which will destroy them, in the mighty name of Jesus.*
4. *Father, I must not take a rest at any location where I will subject my children to torture or violation, in the mighty name of Jesus.*

Something happened not so long ago; life in the UK, is such that the choice of where you live, and settle can affect a lot of things. At the start of the school year many school placements are dependent on your location; there is an invisible line drawn which decides, the catchment area, and your children cannot be admitted into the school if you are outside it, not only that, you cannot have access to any other school there and you cannot register with any GP.

Why are there are so many laws restricting us? Because where you are located decides what you have access to.

We will pray now:

5. Lord, I ask on behalf of myself and my family, any settlement, any placement, that will put my children's life in danger, Father I reject on their behalf, in the mighty name of Jesus.
6. Father direct my children's path away from any placement, any location, oh Lord, that will put them at a disadvantage, in the mighty name of Jesus.
7. Father Lord God Almighty, according to your word, you said the lines are falling unto me in pleasant places and I have a goodly heritage. I decree and I declare Lord, concerning me, concerning my children, I say the lines are falling unto us in pleasant places, in the mighty name of Jesus.
8. Father, i safeguard my children from every good-looking land, that destroys it's inhabitant, in the name of Jesus.
9. I thank you because the steps of the righteous are ordered of God and for this reason, Oh Lord God Almighty, my children's placement is divinely orchestrated.
10. My children and I, my household will settle in a place of advantage,

in the mighty name of Jesus.

The association which took place between Jacob and the people of the land of Shechem was the downfall of Diana - Jacob's daughter.

We are going to pray, and we are going to say:
11. Lord, every association that will lead to the violation of my children, I cancel, and I remove myself from them right now, in the mighty name of Jesus.

If you remember, there is a testimony I shared a while ago. The testimony was shared with us, because we prayed on the forum like this. We prayed that the Lord will open our eyes to whatever was happening in our household. This sister had somebody she had allowed into her home. She was helping another girl; unknown to her that girl was violating her son.

We are going to pray tonight and say:
12. Lord, every association I may be involved in, that will lead to violation of my children, Father, I remove myself and I ask that you forcefully remove me from such the mighty name of Jesus.
13. I refuse to associate with any person, any parties that will lead to the violation of my children, in the mighty name of Jesus.

In the series I shared on thypreciousjewels blog, some of our young girls now married were violated by cousins, friends, family friends, uncles and people who visited their homes.

So, we are going to pray:

14. Lord, every association, every guest coming into my home to stand to violate my children, Father, I shut the door in their faces, in the mighty name of Jesus.
15. I guard my borders in the mighty name of Jesus. I refuse to allow any visitor, association or acquaintance that will violate my children, in the mighty name of Jesus.
16. My children are preserved and secure, in the mighty name of Jesus.

A while ago I thought about some of the things happening in places like America; some convicted criminals are sentenced to death by lethal injection. They have a chair in the gas chamber, and it looks like a normal chair. A person needing a comfortable place to sit will be grateful to see a chair, the only problem is that this chair is not for comfort. The room looks attractive, it looks fine, but remember that is not a normal chair. Upon that chair, several have lost their lives; upon that chair, several have been condemned in eternity.

We are going to pray:

17. Father, the land may look nice, the land may look inviting; every land that will destroy my children, they will not take it, they will not inhabit such land, in the name of Jesus.
18. As many attractive placements, occasions and events, but with the intention to destroy, Father, separate my children from them, in the name of Jesus.
19. Open my eyes Lord and open the eyes of my children; every placement, every location that will affect my children and jeopardize their future, I cancel today, and I reject on their behalf, in

the name of Jesus.

Looking at the story of Jacob, we can see what happened; looking at the story of Lot, we can see also what happened. Lot followed Abraham into the land the Lord directed Abraham. He made the journey with him, but the Bible says that Lot settled near Sodom. For some of our children, the things which will happen to them in life depends on where we settle as parents.

You are going to ask and say:
20. *Lord, open my eyes tonight to see clearly where you have allocated to me to settle.*

Discussing with a pastor friend a while back, she told me about the principalities within an area. When you declare and decree say, 'to bring under subjection to the forces operating in a given area in the mighty name of Jesus.' You do this because there are powers at work. Sometimes, they are in our neighborhood, sometimes they are on our street. People on that street do not progress when this is so.

You are going to pray and say:
21. *Father, wherever my family are located right now, every power at work, that is contrary to the power of the living God, contrary to the covenant of progress He has given for my children, Father I disarm them, in the mighty name of Jesus.*
22. *I decree, the environment is free for my children to prosper. I decree, the air is free for my children to prosper, in the mighty name of Jesus. The environment is free for my children to prosper, in the mighty*

name of Jesus. I decree Lord God Almighty, the air on my street, the air on my road, the air within my premises, they are free. They open directly to heaven.

23. *There shall be no blockage, there shall be no powers to withhold or stand in the way of my prayers, in the mighty name of Jesus. I saturate my street, I saturate the road on which I live, I saturate my premises with the power of the living God in the name of Jesus.*

24. *Every power contrary to that of the living God designed against my children's progress that brings regression, to delay development, I come against you and I pull you down. In the mighty name of Jesus, I decree my children are free to prosper, in this land where the Lord has planted us, in the mighty name of Jesus.*

25. *Lord, you will lead my children as they make the choices, they need to make the choice of school, the choice of friends, the choice of church, the choice of career.*

It's interesting that we need to pray about the choice of church, Yes! There is so much deception out there; we are no longer sure about many of our churches. Some are not built on the Word of God at all. They have all sorts of dark powers making things work within that church. So, you need to pray. You need to carefully decide where your children go. You need to carefully decide who places their hands on them.

You are going to pray and say:

26. *Lord, in the choices of where my children exposure, Father, I receive insight that I will be able to make the right choice and the right deductions, in the mighty name of Jesus.*

27. I will not expose my children to ungodly anointing and laying on of hands, in the mighty name of Jesus.
28. I reject and I refuse for them, every transference of anointing, of spirit that is contrary to that of the living God, in the mighty name of Jesus.
29. Father Lord God Almighty, I secure my children's contact in school. I secure their contact among their friends.
30. I secure their contact even in church they will attend.
31. I secure their contact even in their career, in the mighty name of Jesus.

I shared a story a while ago, while on a flight from Lagos to one European country; a young man on the same flight whom you could see was coming to the UK to study. He reclined his chair and made himself comfortable as soon as he settled into his seat. Behind him was an elderly woman, who stretched her hand from the back and hit him on the head. Everyone turned, looking at the boy, with the elderly woman saying, *"Take your seat up"*, *Take your seat up!"* I was indignant and I ask myself if this boy did not have the same right as the woman; for God's sake, he paid the same fare as everyone else. The boy probably didn't understand what was happening. I considered he was kind of naive because replied the woman saying, *"Leave me alone. I'm free to put my seat like this."* He kept his seat reclined.

This elderly woman began to hit him again and proceeded to swear and curse this boy! At that point, I got so angry within my spirit and I said Lord, *'Where is the mother of this boy?'* The Bible says that a curse without a cause fails. And I hoped, at that moment, that this boy's mother was standing in the gap for her son that night because the type of proclamations and pronouncements the elderly woman made were awful and dreadful. For a sin that was the littlest thing anyone could do, this woman started declaring upon this boy, 'You will not grow old, you will not do this, you will not do that...'. This opened my eyes to see something, there are times our children go to places; times when we are not even aware what they encounter. We are going to be praying now and we shall secure our children ahead of time. They will meet with people; different kinds of people, evil people. We are going to secure our children and we are going to decree and declare that in the mighty name of Jesus:

32. *In the course of my children's journey through life, I shield them from every encounter with evil, in the mighty name of Jesus.*
33. *My children, I shield you from every encounter with evil whether you know about it or you do not know about it. I say you will not encounter evil, in the mighty name of Jesus.*
34. *In your innocence, evil will not chase you. In your innocence, evil will not destroy you. In your innocence, evil will not punish you, in the mighty name of Jesus. I decree and I declare concerning you, my children, I shield you from every evil encounter.*
35. *I shield you from every evil proclamation and pronouncement. I decree my children, you are secure from every talk, every pronouncement, every proclamation that will come unto you from the mouth of evil strangers. I decree that you are secure, in the mighty name of Jesus.*

We know that they may step on toes without knowing; even times they do not mean any harm, but they will step on toes.

You are going to pray right now and say:

36. LORD, every declaration that has been made to the harm and disfavour my children, whether they were made before now or immediately after they were born, I cancel and reverse them right now, in the mighty name of Jesus.
37. I cancel and I reverse every evil proclamation that have been made against my children by evil contacts and evil encounters, in the mighty name of Jesus.
38. I decree Lord God Almighty, as many that will still be made to their disfavour, I cancel and nullify ahead of time, in the might name of Jesus.
39. I decree in the name of Jesus, every evil, proclamation, pronouncement, declaration, that have been made against my children, that have been made to their disfavour, right now, in the name of Jesus, I cancel and I reverse, in Jesus name.
40. In their ignorance, my children will not break the hedge of protection that covers them, in the mighty name of Jesus.

Do you realise that children sometimes, innocently and ignorantly step out of the cover by the words of their mouth. I watched a movie a long time ago; in this movie, one of the single ladies looked at some elderly women seated at a party; as she walked past them, they asked her for food and she turned around and said, *"Hey, did you guys came here for food, is this why you came to the party?"* she didn't realise that she was addressing some evil people; she broke the hedge through the words of her mouth. She could have just said, *"Sorry Madam, I'm not able to help you as I'm also a visitor here."* That way, she would not have stepped into that.

We are going to pray now and say:
41. Lord, I ask that my children will not break the hedge of protection surrounding them, in the mighty name of Jesus. The Bible says, "He that breaks the hedge, the serpent will bite."
42. I put a hedge of protection around my children tonight and Lord, I take away from them the ability and the permission and the freedom to break that hedge, in the name of Jesus.
43. I secure and I fortify the hedge that surrounds and protects them, in the mighty name of Jesus.

The Lord reminded me that our children will feel challenged sometimes through their lives; all life challenges are not evil; therefore, we need to be sure and we need to be sensitive. Some of the challenges they go through in life may be necessary for them to turn out better and stronger, so the Lord will take them to where He wants to take them. Every time I read through the story of Joseph in Potiphar's house, it is obvious that his experience was intended for evil, but the Lord turned it around. The Lord turned the story around for Joseph. Joseph made contact within that prison that enabled him to know how to govern the throne when he was given access.

We are going to pray and say:
44. Lord, every challenge that will come through my children's path in life, designed for them to go through to get to their destination, Father, I receive, oh Lord, grace for them to bear it and grace to go through it.
45. In the mighty name of Jesus, when my children need to go through some challenges to take them where you want them to be, I receive for them, ease, oh Lord God Almighty; in the mighty name of Jesus, they will not faint, they will not grow weak.
46. They will not give up, oh Lord, in the mighty name of Jesus. They will push through and pull through with confidence; whether I am there or not, their hearts will be encouraged, in the mighty name of Jesus.

47.   They will not give up, they will not fall by the wayside, in the mighty name of Jesus.

What happened to Joseph must have made him very sad; a boy without a mother. There was nobody for him to call and say, *'Please pray for me'.* There was nobody to pray for him, he was all alone and the only blood brother he had, was far away. His other siblings were there, living their own lives. They saw Joseph as a threat, they saw him as an enemy and they wanted to destroy him; that was the reason he ended up in the situation where he ended up.

You are going to pray now and say:
48.   Lord, I ask that you surround my children with help. Whatever location they find themselves, when the challenges of life are tough on them, I ask, oh Lord, in the mighty name of Jesus, that you will surround my children with encouragement.
49.   Surround them with support.
50.   Surround them with help, in the mighty name of Jesus. Help will be made available to them, in the name of Jesus.
51.   Father, you will lift up the countenance of my children. They will not be subdued and overwhelmed.
52.   My children will not be depressed or dejected by the challenges meant to raise them up, in the mighty name of Jesus.
53.   They will be strengthened in their inner man. Strength will come, encouragement will come, support will come for my children, in the mighty name of Jesus.

By virtue of Joseph's performance through that short time of trial and tribulation, he proved himself to be an excellent man.

You are going to pray and say,
54.   'Lord, every time my children need to prove themselves in life, before they can access their next level, please Lord, you will give them the

strength.'

Another thing we need to keep minding is that careers are so competitive these days. The present environment is not made for weaklings; if you are weak, you are gone, if you are weak, you will be thrown out without a thought.

Say as you pray:
55. Lord, strengthen the heart of my children. Father Lord God Almighty, make them bold. Give them boldness in their heart to confront the world they have in front of them. They will face their generation with boldness, in the name of Jesus.

Some people are miserable, some are desperate, some dejected; they don't know where to turn to because the environment is challenging. It's going to get even tougher; that's how the Word says it is. It's going to get worse and worse because these are the end times.

You are going to pray today and say:
56. Lord, I pray for boldness for my children. I pray for a strong resolution, oh Lord. My children will not chicken out during difficult times and the pressures of life. Their mind will be strong, in the name of Jesus.
57. The Bible says, **'I've not given you the spirit of fear but that of power, of love and a sound mind.'** I receive for my children sound mind in the name of Jesus. Sound mind to sustain them through competition. Sound mind to sustain them even among their mates at school. Sound mind to be strong in their resolution. They will have a strong resolve to do the right thing, in the mighty name of Jesus.
58. Father, as you place them in distinctive places, they will stand shoulders high. They will not be timid; they will not be shy. They will take the places in life you have prepared and planned for them. We give you glory and honour, in Jesus name.

The Lord asked me to share an experience I went through a few years back; especially for the parents whose children are not able to get into their desired school. Whilst I was waiting to enter secondary school, I wrote exams, and I hoped get admission the best schools at the time. My score was really high and I was invited for the interview; after the interview, a lady called my dad aside and said to my dad, *"You know, you don't really know anybody, do you?"* My Father said, *"No I don't know anybody"* Then she said, *"The way this works, you really have to grease some palms."* My father, being who he was, said, *"I'm so sorry. I will not give a bribe. If my child does not enter this school, she will not die."* And he said to me, "I refuse to bribe anybody; so, if they don't give you any place, that's alright." I did not get a place in that school.

I got into another secondary school and I continued my studies. A few years down the line, my secondary school and the one I was denied entry competed against each other in a televised competition and I won for my school in the final round. The principal of the other school came to me and said, *"Wow, what a brain."* You know what? I didn't let that golden opportunity slide through my fingers even as young as I was. I told the lady, *"My father could not bribe you, but he is still my father, and this is the young girl you rejected several years ago."* The woman looked at me with her mouth agape. There was nothing she could say.

I want to encourage your hearts; it is not the end of the story if your children did not get the placement you desired. If it happens that a flight was delayed, and somebody who was meant to go on that flight missed the flight, and that plane crashed; what would you say? That God has saved them?

You are going to pray and say:
59. *My children may have been cheated out of a position, but I ask, Father, that you will cause them to be celebrated in the places where they have been rejected, in the places where they have been refused.*
60. *Father, you will exalt the horns of my children. There is no location that comes by mistake.*

Even the school the Lord allowed me to go at that time, there was a reason for it, because the Lord trained me in a peculiar way. I am sure I would not have had that exposure. And I'm sure the Lord helped my father to not give that bribe so that they did not destroy and thwart that path God made for my life.

So, I'm begging you today, do not alter the way that the Lord want your children to go. As long as you have prayed for them, support them prayerfully and let the Lord have His way.

You are going to pray and say:
61. Lord, everywhere my children have been rejected, everywhere they have been refused, everywhere they have been disgraced, I decree Lord God Almighty, a season of celebration for them in every one of those places, in the mighty name of Jesus.
62. The Bible says that "**the stones that the builders rejected has now been made a cornerstone**". Every place where my children have met with rejection, I decree Lord, as they knock on doors, those doors shall start to open according to your will, according to your purpose, in the name of Jesus.

For the parents whose children study abroad is delayed due to visa and or sponsorship is the problems.

This is the time to connect and say:
63. Lord, everywhere you have destined for my children to reach, and they are being delayed and rejected, today Lord, I stand on the altar of mercy and I say, as long as this is in your plan for my children, I reverse every negative decision. I reverse every negative judgement and I decree that the borders are open, in the mighty name of Jesus.
64. Father Lord, as long as it is the land you have prepared for my children, I decree access doors and access gates opened in the mighty name of Jesus.
65. Lift up your heads, oh ye gates and let the son of the King of Glory, let the daughter of the King of Glory enter, in the mighty name of Jesus. My children, I decree today, every land the Lord has purposed and planned for you, where you have been rejected so far, I decree open doors, in the mighty name of Jesus. I say, doors be open on your own accord, be open in the name of Jesus. Father, we thank

you, for in Jesus name.

A lady contacted me while ago on THYPRECIOUSJEWELS and said, 'Omo B, we prayed regarding our job at the beginning of the year and I got a message yesterday from and interview I attended 6 months earlier; I was informed at the time of the interview that they will only contact those who made it through the selection process. Not only did they contact me, they I was asked resume with immediate effect." An interview which was done 6 months earlier!

You are going to pray and say:
66. Lord, you that opened the book of remembrance in the Bible, open the book of remembrance to my children, in the name of Jesus. Favour shall start to find them. Wherever you have put them, whatever you have planned for them to be, Father Lord God Almighty, whether I know it or not, I say let the knock of favour start to come. Let the letters of favour start to come. Let the phone calls of favour start to come, in the mighty name of Jesus.
67. Every divine placement you have allocated to my children being inhabited by others, i command that unlawful occupants vacate the seat that belongs to my children, in the mighty name of Jesus. I say, doors be opened, in the mighty name of Jesus. I decree free access for my children.

I want us to pray this last prayer point.
There are times when you as the parent pray and the children have no clue what you are praying about. They keep messing about; they keep wasting money, they keep wasting resources. A friend shared something with me not so long ago about a young person. They kept changing their university course; they made the changes after they'd spent about a year. Resources were being wasted; time was being wasted. When other children were about to graduate, this child was still wondering about what to do.

Ask now that the Lord:
68. Will give your children insight into their journey through life. Ask that the Lord will give them insight into where they are going. When

a child has focus, your journey is easy as a mother. You do not have to chase them about or ask them to, 'Go and read your books.' No! This is because that child already has eyes for great things. That child has his eyes on greatness and you just need to push a little bit and he will come on top.

You are going to pray and say:
69. Lord, open my children's eyes, let them see the greatness you have ahead of them. Help them to see the greatness you have prepared for them. Help them to see the greatness of where you are taking them.
70. Father give my children insight, oh Lord, that they will not walk around aimlessly. That I will not be the one to push them. They will not wander around aimlessly. They will not go to locations that will waste their life. They will not go to locations that will waste what you have deposited inside of them.
71. Father, my children will receive motivation, of their own accord. Regarding their future, they are motivated. Regarding their career, they are motivated. Regarding married life, they are motivated. Regarding their health, they are motivated. In every aspect of life, my children are motivated, in the mighty name of Jesus.

I want to encourage your hearts, because sometimes, it is as though your child will only prosper in a specific place. Your children need to go to the school that is God's plan and purpose for them.

You are going to pray to and say:
72. Lord, I ask that you will correct my life; that I will know where I need to send my children. Concerning the choice of school, you will give me insight as to the choice of where to live.

Some families would need to change location of and accommodation, because that was the beginning of the problem you are experiencing. Your children look around you and all they can see is failure; they are not motivated to go through life.

Pray and say:
73.	Lord, I ask that you give me a divine placement, give me a divine relocation so that what my children see around them will be motivational, not something to drag them down, in the mighty name of Jesus.
74.	Father, I pray, I ask, oh Lord God Almighty, that you open the eyes of my children to see the great life you have ahead of them. Father, because of this, they will work hard, they will push themselves in the direction you want them to go.
75.	When a child does not get a befitting result for their labour, they become discouraged. LORD, my children's efforts will not be wasted. I will not waste their efforts. I will not expose them to situations, circumstances, friendship and contact that will destroy them.

Father, we give you all the glory; we thank you because you have heard us, for in Jesus name we have prayed.

CONCLUSION

Our Father and our God, we want to thank you for a time like this. Thank You, Lord, because you hear us always. You have asked for us to pray concerning our children. We thank you, Lord God Almighty, because you are the one who plants us by the rivers of water, and we bring forth our fruit in due season. Father for myself, for all my sisters and brothers who are connected to this prayer call today, I am asking, oh Lord, in the name of Jesus, for divine planting. It is only when we are planted that we are rooted. It is only when we are rooted that we can bear fruit in due season. I ask oh Lord, for divine planting, in the name of Jesus.

As many as are planted in the wrong place, by the wrong people and circumstances of life, I ask, oh Lord, for supernatural relocation, in the name of Jesus. I ask, oh Lord. peradventure we planted ourselves in places you have not approved of, Father I ask by your mighty hand, remove us forcefully and plant us in the right places you have prepared for our children, in the name of Jesus. Father, I ask tonight for every one of us; as many of us as have planted ourselves in contact with people, with persons, who will violate our children, who will disgrace our children, Father, build a wall of separation between us and those unlawful contacts and ungodly contact, in the name of Jesus. Peradventure they are in our household, Father, we uproot them by the power in the name of Jesus. And we decree Lord God Almighty, that you will give us insight to protect these children from and keep them away from oppressors.

Father Lord, there are so many evil people around, and at times our children ignorantly and naively speak anyhow, they behave anyhow. They laugh anyhow. I ask, oh Lord, that you will shield our children from evil encounters, in the name of Jesus. With their words, actions and attitudes, they will not offend evil, in the name of Jesus. Father Lord God Almighty, I put around my children and the children of all my sisters and brothers who are connected to this prayer line, I surround them with the hedge of protection and I say Lord, by their hand, they will not break this hedge of protection you have put around them, in the mighty name of Jesus.

Father we give you glory, and we give you honour. Thank you, Lord, because everywhere our children have been disgraced, humiliated and rejected, I decree a season of celebration for them, in the mighty name of Jesus. As many as are looking up to you because they know and they are sure you have sent their children on divine placement to countries far away, I am connecting with them today, Lord. and I ask that the doors be open, in the name of Jesus. As many of them as have been denied, rejected, refused and humiliated, Father I ask, in the same place where they have been refused and humiliated, we decree favour in the name of Jesus. Doors will open to them of their own accord, in the name of Jesus. We give you glory tonight because you have heard us, for in Jesus name we have prayed.

Amen! Thank you very much.

Chapter 5
SALVATION

In this chapter, we are going to be praying concerning two separate aspects: our children's salvation and their prosperity. We start by reading:

Genesis 39:6-10 (CJB)
So, he left all his possessions in Yosef's* care; and because he had him, he paid no attention to his affairs, except for the food he ate. Now Yosef* was well-built and handsome as well. (vi) [7] In time, the day came when his master's wife took a look at Yosef* and said, "Sleep with me!" [8] But he refused, saying to his master's wife, "Look, because my master has me, he doesn't know what's going on in this house. He has put all his possessions in my charge. [9] In this house I am his equal; he hasn't withheld anything from me except yourself, because you are his wife. How then could I do such a wicked thing and sin against God?" [10] But she kept pressing him, day after day. Nevertheless, he didn't listen to her; he refused to sleep with her or even be with her.

The Bible says as it turned out, God was with Joseph and things went very well with him; he went on living in the home of his Egyptian Master. His master recognized that God was with him, such that God worked for good in everything he did. The Bible says that the master became very fond of Joseph and made him his personal aide; he put him in charge of his personal affairs turning everything over to him. From that moment onwards, God blessed the home of the Egyptian all because of Joseph; the blessing of God spread over everything he owned at home and in the field. The Bible says that all Potiphar had to concern himself with was eating 3 meals. As a strikingly handsome young man, Joseph's master's wife became infatuated with and one day said, *"Sleep with me..."* The Bible says that he wouldn't do it. He said to his master's wife, *"With me here, my master doesn't give a second thought to anything that goes on here. He has put me in charge of everything he owns. He treats me as an equal. The only thing he hasn't turned over to me is you. You are his wife after all. How can I violate his trust and sin against God?"* The bible accounts that Potiphar's wife continued to pester Joseph.

Today, the Lord wants us to pray concerning our children's salvation. We know the story - how Joseph ended up in Potiphar's house. His brothers planned against him.

Our first prayer is:

1. Lord, please save my children from every circumstance and situation in life that will put my children in a position to sin against you. Save them Lord from every such situation, even before it comes into existence, in the name of Jesus.
2. Father, I bring my children before you. Lord God Almighty, you know the story of their lives, you know the path on which they will walk. You know the offices in which they will work; you know the friends they will keep. Father, I pray today, Lord, ahead of time: every situation, every circumstance, oh Lord, that will put them in the position to sin against you, Father deliver them from now, In the mighty name of Jesus.

3. *Father Lord God Almighty, the path of the youth is very slippery. Save them Lord God Almighty even from relationships, from experiences, from acquaintances; from circumstances and from situations that will put them in a position to sin against you. Deliver them even before that experience comes, oh Lord, in the mighty name of Jesus.*

The Bible says in: **Proverbs 27:12**
"A wise man seeth trouble far away and avoids it."

Father, I pray for my children today:
4. *I start to redirect the course of your life away from iniquity and anything that will turn you against God in the mighty name of Jesus. I decree that the Lord will release the ability and wisdom to walk right, in Jesus name.*

The Bible says, "How can a man keep his ways except the Lord?" Living for the Lord is not easy; we all know it. What people do sometimes make you just wonder. Some are working in a bank, and are changing numbers, committing all sorts of fraud; others assume that they have to follow the crowd in lies make it through. Our children are going to face more serious situations than we are face at present, because they would work with are unbelievers - they do not honour the Lord at all.

We are going to pray and say:
5. *Lord, preserve my children from error. Preserve my son from error.*

Preserve my daughter from error, in the name of Jesus. Father save them by your mighty hand. Choose these ones and select them onto you, that they will not put their hand in iniquity or sin. Sin destroys.

6. *Lord, my children must be preserved in you. My children will choose to stand in righteousness, rather than to give in to the desires of the flesh. My children will serve you wholeheartedly. My children will love you with the whole of their heart, oh Lord, in the mighty name of Jesus.*

When Joseph had the offer to sin against God, his parents of Joseph were not there; his siblings were not there and his Pastor was not there. Yet he decided he was not going to give in to the lust of the flesh. The truth is that nobody will ever find out if he had committed that sin, and he would have continued to do that with Potiphar's wife and by that, he will compromise his future.

Pray now and Say:

7. *Lord, secure my children. By yourself, save them from iniquity. Whether it remains a little for them to walk into sin, into error, Father, save them by your mighty hand. Let somebody walk in. Let something make them uncomfortable. Father, this is what I desire for my children. Save them by any means oh Lord. Save my children from error. Save them from iniquity. Save them from sin, oh Lord, in the mighty name of Jesus. Father, this is my prayer this day.*

*The Bible says in **Psalm 125:3***

"The wicked rod will not remain in the land given to the righteous, so that they will not put their hand to do that which is wrong".

Joseph found himself in a 'wrong' place, how did that happen? His brothers led him to it because they hated him.

We are going to pray and say:

8. Lord, so that my children will not sin against you, so that my children will not find themselves in a wrong place, direct their path in life. Every path you have not ordained for my children, Father, I refuse for them to walk through it, in the name of Jesus.

When you find yourself in the wrong place, wrong things have no choice but to happen.

Pray and Say:

9. Father, my children will not find themselves in or with the wrong company. They will not find themselves with the wrong friends. They will not find themselves in the wrong job. They will not find themselves in the wrong location, in the mighty name of Jesus.

10. Father, I secure my children and their path in life. I say they will not find themselves in a position that will make them to sin against God, in the mighty name of Jesus. They will not find themselves in the midst of friends, men or women who will make them to sin against you, in the mighty name of Jesus we have prayed.

Some of parents handed their children over to the pastors of the church to dedicate. It is important you by yourself take your children before the Lord, whether or not these children have been brought to church dedication. Dedicate your children to the Lord right now, whether the pastor put salt or pepper or water in their mouth; because you are the one who gave birth to them, during childbirth, you poured your blood upon them, you fed them from your bosom, you are going to bring them before the altar of God now and lay them there, saying:

11. *Father, this seed that came out of my body, I dedicate this seed to you. Take over their lives and their hearts. Father, I decree that my children will know you. My children will serve you. My children will walk perfect before you. Lord, I dedicate my children to you. In the whole of their lives, they will choose you. In the whole of their lives, they will serve you. Father, I commit my children unto you. I say Lord, my children will serve you. My children will love you. My children will know you. My children will walk perfect before you, in the name of Jesus.*

12. *Lord, whatever altar my children were dedicated on before now, Father Lord God Almighty, I bring them before you afresh and anew. I say my son will serve you. Wholeheartedly, he will know you. He will work perfect before you, in the name of Jesus. My daughter will honour you. My daughter will know you for herself oh Lord, in the name of Jesus. The Bible says that my children will be taught of the Lord. I decree and I declare, I say my daughter, you are taught of the Lord in the name of Jesus. You know the Lord and you walk perfect before Him, in the name of Jesus. I decree over you my son; you will know the Lord and you will not walk in error. In Jesus name.*

It is very easy for you to pray for prosperity for your children when they are walking right before the Lord.

We are going to be praying from
> Isaiah 58:7 (CJB)
>
> sharing your food with the hungry, taking the homeless poor into your house, clothing the naked when you see them, fulfilling your duty to your kinsmen!" [8] Then your light will burst forth like the morning, your new skin will quickly grow over your wound; your righteousness will precede you, and ADONAI's* glory will follow you. [9] Then you will call, and ADONAI* will answer; you will cry, and he will say, "Here I am." If you will remove the yoke from among you, stop false accusation and slander, [10] generously offer food to the hungry and meet the needs of the person in trouble; then your light will rise in the darkness, and your gloom become like noon. [11] ADONAI* will always guide you; he will satisfy your needs in the desert, he will renew the strength in your limbs; so that you will be like a watered garden, like a spring whose water never fails. [12] You will rebuild the ancient ruins, raise foundations from ages past, and be called "Repairer of broken walls, Restorer of streets to live in."

That is the purpose of God for a child who is walking in righteousness. We are going to pray every one of these prayer points.

13. You my child, as you walk before the Lord, your light shall be turned on and your life shall receive a turn-around from now, in the name of Jesus. I pray for you, my children, as you start to honour the Lord.

14. As you start to walk upright before the Lord, I decree that as your light shall be turned on, the righteousness you walk in will pave a way for you. I decree concerning you my son: righteousness will make a way for you in life in the mighty name of Jesus.
15. Righteousness will make your path to be smooth because you will honour the Lord, and because you will walk blameless before the Lord, righteousness will go before you. It will make the path that is inaccessible to others to be accessible to you, in the mighty name of Jesus. Your path will be smooth. I decree concerning you my daughter, when you pray, the Lord will answer. When you call out, the Lord will help you. He will say here I am.
16. As you get rid of unfair practices, the wisdom of the Lord will be your portion to lay hold on to the riches of this world, in the mighty name of Jesus.
7. I declare to you my children, as you walk in righteousness, the riches of the wicked - the riches that belong to you that is in the hand of the wicked - will be restored onto you, in the mighty name of Jesus.

The Bible says, when you are generous with the hungry and you start giving yourself out, your life will begin to glow in the darkness. I speak unto you my children:

18. Your life will glow in darkness. When everybody is saying that the times are hard, you will be smiling. You will be refreshed, in the name of Jesus.
19. The Bible says, your shadowed life will be bathed in sunlight. This I decree concerning you my children.
20. As you walk blameless before the Lord, everywhere that there has been shadow, everywhere that there has been thirst, in the name of Jesus, you will be watered.
21. When people are looking and they cannot find help, wherever you go, help will come to you my children, in the name of Jesus.
22. My children, help will come to you in every area. Every door of greatness and advancement you knock on will be opened to you in

favour, in the name of Jesus. Where people are looking for favour and they are being turned down, you will walk in and the Lord will give you favour, in the mighty name of Jesus. I decree these concerning you, my son and my daughter, in the mighty name of Jesus.

The Bible says, the Lord will show you increase everywhere you go.

23. Your life will be full even in the emptiest of places. I say when people are traveling and relocating and they are saying that the land is awful and they are saying the land is bad, when you reach there, my children, the land will produce its fruit for you. It will yield its fruit for you, in the might name of Jesus. I decree and I declare according to the Word of the Lord in **Isaiah 58: 11, which says 'You will be like a well-watered garden**. You will be a fresh spring that never runs dry', in the name of Jesus.

24. I speak unto you my children, you will never run dry. You will bring forth your fruit in due season. I speak unto my son and daughter you will never run dry and you will bring forth your fruit in due season, in the name of Jesus.

The Bible says concerning you my children, 'You will use old rubbles of past life to rebuild a new one'.

25. You will rebuild foundation from out of your past. You will be known as those who can fix anything. I speak unto you my children, every foundation meant to be active, but has been lying fallow, today, in the name of Jesus, as you dedicate your life and I dedicate you before the altar of the Lord, I say your foundation will start to yield fatness. Your foundation will start to yield smoothness. Your foundation will start to yield milk and honey, in the name of Jesus. I speak concerning you my children.

26. I say you are bringing forth your fruit in this season because you are planted in the courts of the Lord. You flourish in the vines of the Lord.

27. You will not experience delay or drought at any point in your life because your life has been given to Christ, in the name of Jesus.

Some people performed well in nursery, primary, secondary schools; they were remembered but a few years later at the school reunion, you observe that things turned out worse for them.

We are going to pray and say:
28. Lord at every point in my children's lives, because I have brought them before the altar of God today and we have dedicated them, and because the Bible says that the path of the righteous shines brighter and brighter unto the perfect day, I speak unto you my children: you will not know a better yesterday, in the name of Jesus. Your primary school will be better than nursery. Your secondary school will be better than your primary school. Your University will be better than Secondary. Your working life will be better than your University in the mighty name of Jesus. Your path will only shine brighter. Your light will only shine brighter, in the name of Jesus.
29. When people look at you in old age, when people look at you when you start to work, they will look at you and they will say, "Wow! We did not know you could be this good", because the hand of the Lord will lift you up. He will single you out.
30. My children, i decree that the Lord will make you known. He will make you prosperous, in the name of Jesus.
31. In the history of our family, there will be none that can be compared unto you in the name of Jesus, because the Lord will establish you. The Lord will give you fatness for food. He will give you fatness in the place of work. He will give you fatness in your family. He will give you fatness even in the seed that shall come out of your body, in the mighty name of Jesus.
32. Father Lord, I thank you for my children. Thank you, oh Lord God Almighty, because the path that you have set for them will shine brighter and brighter. I speak into my children today: your path will

shine brighter, in the mighty name of Jesus. As you walk before the Lord, he will make you prosperous. He will establish your land. He will make your root go deep into the ground, in the name of Jesus. He will establish you in the work of your hand, in the fruit of your body, even in the ministry he has committed into your hands, in the name of Jesus.

33. *The Bible says, "Though your beginning was small, your latter end shall greatly increase." He says, "You shall wax great and go forward and grow until you become great." This I decree for my children in Jesus name.*

34. *I speak unto you my daughter. I speak unto you my son. Your beginning looks small now. The Bible says your latter end shall greatly increase. You shall wax great. You shall go forward. You shall grow until you become great. Your name shall be known. For righteousness, your name shall be known. In the course that you have chosen, in the career you have chosen, in the ministry the Lord has given to you, you shall be known.*

35. *My children, your name shall be prosperous. Your name shall be established. Your roots will go deep into the ground. You shall yield many fruits in the name of Jesus.*

36. *I declare regarding you my children, you shall not be uprooted prematurely. The Lord will establish you. I speak unto you my son, I speak to you my daughter and I decree and I declare that your roots shall grow deep right into the soil, into the land which the Lord has planted you in and you shall grow tall, as you grow reaching towards heaven - reaching every potentials that God has planned for you, in the mighty name of Jesus.*

37. *As you grow, you shall spread abroad, in the mighty name of Jesus. I decree and I declare concerning you my children, your portion is great in the land of the living. In the career that you have chosen, you will be established. You will prosper, in the name of Jesus. You will be known. The Lord will make your name to be spread abroad.*

Jesus did good - he did wonderful and marvelous things and his name was spread abroad. I decree concerning you, my son, that your name will be spread abroad as the Lord works righteousness through you and as He prospers you in your chosen career. I speak unto my daughter, that the work of your hands shall prosper, and your name shall spread abroad, in the name of Jesus.

> **Let us read Job 22:23-30**
> *If you return to the Almighty you will be built up; if you remove injustice far from your tents, ²⁴ if you lay gold in the dust, and gold of Ophir among the stones of the torrent-bed, ²⁵ then the Almighty will be your gold and your precious silver. ²⁶ For then you will delight yourself in the Almighty and lift up your face to God. ²⁷ You will make your prayer to him, and he will hear you, and you will pay your vows. ²⁸ You will decide on a matter, and it will be established for you, and light will shine on your ways. ²⁹ For when they are humbled you say, 'It is because of pride';[c] but he saves the lowly. ³⁰ He delivers even the one who is not innocent, who will be delivered through the cleanness of your hands."*

Looking at the current situation of things in Nigeria, while people are crying that things are tight, some are still flourishing in the midst of that.

We are going to pray about it and decree about our children that:

38. No matter which country of the world they are located, when people are saying there is casting down, our children will say there is exaltation.
39. My children's testimony will be that there is prosperity. My children's testimony will be that there is plenty. Father I decree and I

declare today.

40. *Father, I decree concerning my children, when the world will be saying there is austerity, my children will be flourishing, oh Lord. When the world will be saying there is nothing, Lord, my children will be giving to the poor. When the world will be saying that there is not enough, my children will be feeding those who are homeless. When the people are saying there is nothing up, my children will have enough to live on and enough to be a blessing to many.*

41. *Father Lord God Almighty, it does not matter the land where they decide to live. It doesn't matter the location where you direct them, Lord, there will enough for them to live on. There will be plenty for them to prosper. There will be enough for them to feed the poor; there will be enough for them to house the homeless, in the mighty name of Jesus.*

42. *Father Lord God Almighty, I decree and I declare, oh Lord, as we have heard in your Word where you said, "They will decree a thing where it shall be established unto them', my children shall decree righteousness and it shall be established unto them. As they call upon you, Lord they will be heard. My children will not be praying prayers that do not have answers; when they speak until you, you will remember my prayer today and you will answer them. You will hearken unto them with speed. Lord, when they cry unto you in distress, you will look with favour upon them, in the mighty name of Jesus.*

43. *Father Lord God Almighty, when they do not know which way to take; when they do not know which choice to make, Father, you will answer my children. Even before they cry, oh Lord, you will hear them. Father, you will remember my cry to you today and you will answer my children. You will remember the time of prayer this day and you will open doors that have been shut unto them.*

44. *Father Lord, you said, "When they make prayers to you, you will hear them, and they will pay their vows." Father Lord God Almighty, I bring my son and my daughter before you today; I say Lord, you will*

hear them. When they cry, you will hear them. When they pray, you will hear them. Even when they whisper, you will hear them. When they talk, you will hear them, in the mighty name of Jesus. As they cry out onto you, Lord, in their time of need, you will answer them. You will look with mercy from Zion and you will favour them. In Jesus name we have prayed.

There are people whose prospering in the world is taking them away from the Lord.

We are going pray; we are going to ask, and we are going to say:
45. "Lord, as my children start to prosper, the prosperity must not take them away from you. Eternally, I give them to you. They will not be able to take themselves out from you. Peradventure they wander, by your hand of strength, we bring them back to you, Lord. By all means, you will save my children.
46. Father Lord God Almighty, the arrows of this world are deceitful, but Lord, you will save my children and by all means. Their prosperity will not take them away from you. The riches you will give them, oh Lord, will not take them away from you, in the mighty name of Jesus. Father, they will be righteous and prosperous. At the same time, they will flourish in the courts of the Lord, in the mighty name of Jesus. Father, these ones will be relevant in your kingdom. Their prosperity will be relevant to you, in the mighty name of Jesus.

CONCLUSION

I thank you Father because you have prospered my children. I give you all the glory and all the honour. Thank you, father, because your word works for my children. Thank you, Father, because as they lay hold on your Word, it comes through for them, in the mighty name of Jesus.

Our Father and our God we want to thank you for today and this time of prayer. Thank you Lord God Almighty because our children's paths are in your hands. Father, we know that no man receives anything unless he *be given from above. Father, prosperity comes from you. Promotion comes from you; Father, I stand in agreement with my children and we decree, oh Lord, that our children are saved, in the name of Jesus. We say when the time shall come for our children to choose, they will willingly and gracefully choose to serve the Lord, in the name of Jesus.*

The Bible says righteousness exalts a nation, but sin is a reproach unto the people. Because our children are righteous, Father, we decree that they are exalted in the land and in their generation, in Jesus name. Father Lord, we have decreed, and we have declared that our children are prosperous in the work of their hand and in the ministries, you will commit unto them. In the fruit of their bodies also, they are prosperous. We decree it is so in the name of Jesus. We thank you Lord for this and we thank you for the answers to our prayers. We give you all the glory Lord, for in Jesus name we have prayed.

Amen

Chapter 6
SAFETY

The Lord has instructed that we pray concerning our children's safety, so we shall be praying for their protection in this chapter. The Lord brought three different scenarios to my attention; has asked me to share them with you.

This is an experienced I had about two weeks ago; while watching a TV documentary about an 11-year-old boy; he was the only child of his parents. Nothing was wrong with him, but his parents noticed that he was not performing as well as they expected in school. They decided to him assessed; after which he was given a diagnosis. They were told that he had *"attention deficiency syndrome"*; they took him to see a child psychiatrist who decided to start him on a very common medication for the condition. This boy got better within the first few weeks of the medication, but do you know what happened? They went back for a refill of the medication at the end of the first month, the pharmacist gave them a different medication in error from what he had the first time; it was a mistake on the part of the pharmacist. He became unwell, he got weaker and weaker. They took him to the hospital. The hospital - the team at the hospital could not find out what was wrong with him; eventually, one day, the parents woke up and they found him dead. They decided that they were going to do an autopsy for this boy the cause of his death as it was not clear. Do you know what they found out? They found out the repeat prescription by the pharmacist, was a dangerous medication, not the one the doctor prescribed. This child died; his life was wasted. The parents gave him the medication that killed him because of the mistake of the chemist.

We are going to pray:
1. Lord, my children will not suffer as a result of somebody else's error. I refuse to let go of my child's life and their future because of

somebody's mistake. Lord, I refuse!!!
2. Father in the name of Jesus, I bring my seeds before you tonight. I stand on this altar of mercy today and I pray concerning my children: **THEY WILL NOT SUFFER!**
3. Lord, wherever my children will go Lord God Almighty, let your eyes of mercy and favour follow them.
4. Be it the food they eat or the water they drink; even when we go out for a meal oh Lord, their food shall not be poisoned. Father Lord God Almighty, the water they are offered at school shall not be contaminated. My children will not run into distress.
5. Father, this is my declaration and my proclamation today: in the morning, afternoon and night, you will save them from human error. You will save them from human mistakes oh Lord. Father, this is my proclamation concerning my seed.
6. My children will not die untimely death because of professional incompetence.

Some people at times go into a hospital with a simple complaint but come back with something worse. I have seen it so many times.

We are going to pray and say:
7. Lord, every simple sickness that will be magnified as a result of visit to the doctor, the chemist or people who are supposed to help, I prevent such from the beginning in the mighty name of Jesus. I say such will not feature in my children's body in the mighty name of Jesus.
8. Father Lord, I speak into my children's body this day: my son, you will be in peace. Your body will be in peace. I speak concerning you my daughter: your body will be in peace. Every simple disease, every

simple illness, every simple complaint that will be complicated and turned into something big, Father, in the name of Jesus, I bind them from my children's body.
9. *I disallow every simple day to day illnesses that will magnify into something extraordinary. I bind them from the beginning, in the mighty name of Jesus. I say they have no place to dwell in my children's body. Sickness and disease have no root to plant in their body. I speak today and I decree that you are protected and preserved from invasion and from every one of these oppressions, in the mighty name of Jesus.*

There are all sorts of diseases, illnesses and disorders of both the mind and the body. During my practice, I saw this child of about ten years old. When I asked the parents, "Why am I seeing your child?", they said, *"He keeps hearing voices of somebody saying they are going to kill him."* That is a disorder of the mind; it doesn't matter what medication you treat that child with. He was already hearing voices of strange people at the age of 9. Can you imagine what will happen to him by the time he is 30?

We are going to pray tonight and say:
10. "Lord, I present the bodies of my children to you; they will not entertain any abnormal thoughts. My children's minds will function perfectly, in the mighty name of Jesus. My son, my daughter, your minds are intact; your souls are intact, and your bodies are intact.
11. Father, I speak concerning my children. I rebuke every disorder of the mind. I rebuke every disorder of the soul. I rebuke every torture of the body, in the mighty name of Jesus.
12. Oh, you seed of my body, I decree that it is well with your mind, in

the mighty name of Jesus. It is well with your soul. It is well with your spirit in Jesus name.

Many of us take things that happens to us physically for granted; they never happen on their own. There is always a spiritual reason and an undertone.

We are therefore, going to pray now and say:

13. *Lord, peradventure there is a destruction that has been assigned to my children in the youth of their life, today in the name of Jesus, I remove such from their path in life and I proclaim that they shall not be cut short. They shall not be wasted, in the name of Jesus.*

I stand this day with the hand of God upon my life and the altar on which I pray and I decree: Lord, every destruction contracted to destroy my children in the prime and the youth of their lives, in the mighty name of Jesus, today, I remove such destruction from their source. I remove it from their path, now and in the future.

14. *Every destruction set and timed at particular times of their lives - some are timed to come when they are 9, some when they are 15, or 35 or even when they are older; every destruction timed for the future of my children, today I break that appointment, in the mighty name of Jesus. Every appointment set to destroy my children, their mind, their body, soul and spirit, I break them today from my children's life.*

15. *Every appointment with destiny that is not in line with the spirit of God, I cancel today in the mighty name of Jesus. I decree, you shall not go through. I decree that you shall not proceed with it. Today, I*

mark the end of it, in the mighty name of Jesus. As the second goes and the minute goes and the hour goes, I put an end to you, in the mighty name of Jesus we have prayed.

Still on the documentary I was watched, another frightening scenario ensued; it was raining when the children got on the to go home after school; these children decided to get off the bus, all of them in one place. The tallest one among them, a 10-year old girl said, *'Because I'm the tallest, I will hold the umbrella to cover the four of us."* As she held the umbrella and cover the four of them thunder struck just a few steps from the bus. It went straight for the girl that holding the umbrella; the other three girls ran as they heard that noise and the tall girl, the one holding the umbrella to cover everyone else, was hit and she died there and then. She was burned, she went into cardiac arrest. Why? Because she was protecting others.

We are going to pray and say:

16. *Lord, every power that destroys in the noon; every power that destroys in the morning, that comes out of nowhere to take out life, Father, I bind and I ban them from operating in my children's life, in the name of Jesus. Every power that wastes in the middle of the day, I refuse you from operating in my children's life.*
17. *Father, I stand upon the rock of ages and upon the altar of Jesus Christ today and decree: every power that destroys suddenly, in the mighty name of Jesus, you will not come near my seeds. Every power that wastes during the day, you will not come near my seeds. Every power that frustrates life out of children, every power that causes parents to go into sudden sorrow, I refuse you from our lives. I refuse you from my children's body. Everything that causes a sudden*

destruction, you will not come near my children. My children are safe from any sudden destruction, in the mighty name of Jesus.

That 10-year old girl had the heart to serve others; the minute she fell, one of the girls she was covering with the umbrella ran to call her mother, but it was too late by the time she got there.

We are going to pray and say:
18. Lord, today I stand on the altar of Jesus Christ. I refuse every sudden negative news - every sudden sad news, I refuse in the name of Jesus!
19. Father I stand on the altar of Jesus Christ today and I decree concerning my seeds; I shall not welcome and heartbreaking report or news regarding my children.
20. Every sad news, every sudden sad news, every news from anywhere that is unpleasant regarding my children, I refuse them, Lord. I refuse to entertain any sad news from my children, concerning my children, about my children. Thank you, Lord, because you've heard. We give you all the glory Lord. In Jesus name.

If we look at what happened to that girl, her height was the cause of her death; she opted to help cover others because she was taller.

We are going to pray and say:
21. Lord, I refuse to allow the goodness I see in my children, the goodness other people see in my children to be their downfall.

Some children may talented singers; and through that they get noticed. Some get jealous of the child and before you know it, they begin to plan to harm them.

So, we shall pray now and say:
22. Lord the goodness I see in my child is causing me joy, I refuse for them to be the downfall of my child, in the mighty name of Jesus. You will preserve them through the beautiful features you've given unto them, in the mighty name of Jesus.

In Psalm 57:1,
Be merciful unto me, O God, be merciful unto me: for my soul trusteth in thee: yea, in the shadow of thy wings will I make my refuge, until these calamities be overpast.

DECLARE:
23. Lord, peradventure there is evil ahead, you to delay my seed. My children will never catch up with the evil ahead. And peradventure Lord, evil is coming from behind, You, oh Lord, will order their steps swiftly only towards safety. You will hasten them up so that the evil coming from behind will not catch up with them.

A while ago, as a young girl, still in primary school near closing time, which would be about 2 o'clock in the afternoon. While many of us students walked home, a truck lost control on a hill in the village and went straight into the marketplace. Many mothers sent their children to the market to buy food stuff as it was on their way home. Some children were killed by that truck in their school uniforms; one of them, a very close family friend of mine. To break the news to her mum, my sister and my mum had to bring her mum to our home and the news was broken to this woman in my house. They later went to find the remains of this girl who went to school in the morning, left school in the afternoon but never got home. She was crushed to death in her school uniform. That girl would have missed that calamity had left school twenty minutes later or earlier.

We are going to pray and say:
24. Lord, every calamity going ahead, delay my children. They must not catch up with them.
25. Every calamity coming from behind, hasten my children so the calamity will not meet up with them.
26. Father I come before the altar of mercy today, I know calamities will always happen; evil will always happen in this world, but I ask, Lord, that you preserve my seeds, in the name of Jesus.
27. Father, the evil coming ahead will not meet my children; when the evil is coming from behind, you will hasten their steps, oh Lord, in the mighty name of Jesus. Thank you, father, because You have heard us, in Jesus name.

A child who does not sleep at night, will also keep his parents from sleeping. The Lord gave me a word in **Psalm 4:8**. It says: "I will lay down in peace and sleep, for the Lord makes me dwell in safety".

I want us to pray for our children to be able to sleep at night. Scientifically, it is proven that a child with a poor sleeping habit will have poor performance during the day. A lot of things can take away sleep from our children; if your child has problem in this area, please pay attention.

You are going to decree:
28. My child, at night, you will not be an object of attack.
29. At night, you will lay down in peace and you will sleep. Your sleep shall be peaceful, and it shall be restful. Father, I stand in the gap concerning my children tonight. I say sleep cannot be a problem or challenge for you, my son, my daughter. Your sleep shall be sweet and refreshing, it shall not be destroyed. Your night shall be peaceful and your day restful, in the mighty name of Jesus.

  I want us to use Psalm 91 for our children. We are going to pray, decree and declare concerning your children, the seed of your womb.
30. Concerning you, the seed of my womb, the Lord will keep you safe from every secret trap and every deadly disease in Jesus name.
31. Concerning you my children, the Lord will preserve you; He will protect you; He will keep you safe from every secret trap, in the mighty name of Jesus.
32. The lord will protect you from every deadly disease and preserve you such that no evil will come near your dwelling place, which is your body.

  The Bible says in **Psalm 91**: He will spread His wings over you and keep you secure.

Pray now and say:
33. Lord, you will spread your wings over my children and keep them secure. Whether I am with them or not, Lord you will secure my children. Spread your wings over my children, Lord, in the morning, afternoon and night. This is their portion, Father. Under your wings, they will stay, and they will sleep and wake daily, in Jesus name.

  Psalm 91:7
  The Bible says, a thousand may fall at your right and ten thousand at your left, but they will not come near you. Only with your eyes shall you see the reward of the wicked.

We are going to pray and say:
34. Lord, it doesn't matter what calamity is befalling children, I decree that my children must not be partakers of this.
35. I secure my children. The Bible says that the lots of the wicked shall not fall on the righteous. I say Lord God Almighty, whatever calamity, whatever disease, whatever pandemonium happening

around, they will not come near my children; my children will be preserved.
36. Father, as they go to school, they are preserved. As they wake up in the morning, they are preserved. When they play at the playground, they are preserved. Father, in class, they are preserved. At home, they are preserved. As they walk on the streets, travel in cars, fly in the air, travel through waters and even on modes of transportations that have not yet been discovered, My seeds are preserved all through the hour, all through the day in the mighty name of Jesus.

I shared an experience with some sisters recently; a few years ago, a little girl was playing around our house during which she had an insect bite. There was nothing unusual with insect bites; she had a little swelling, other than that, nothing significant. The young girl came in; she told the parents and said, *"Mummy see."* They had a look at the insect bite, put Robb, a balm, on it; but by that evening the entire hand was swollen and the parents, thought *"Wow, that's unusual! Okay, but it is going to get better tomorrow."* They gave her some pain relief and the child went to bed with some antihistamine. By the time she woke up the next day, the whole of the arm was swollen; also, the whole of her body was swollen by next evening. The parents did not realize was that it was a dangerous insect. Six weeks down the line, her blood level was very low. In fact, the parents thought they were going to lose this child because she had become heavily anemic. A simple insect bite destroyed this girl's kidneys, unable to produce blood cells; she died within 8 weeks of the insect bit - a child that was not unwell in any way.

PLEASE PRAY:
37. Lord, from every accident, every injury, every trap set, no matter what the source is, Lord, secure my children in Jesus name.
38. Every simple insult and injury the enemy hides under to destroy destinies, will not find my children in the name of Jesus.

39. I speak concerning my children; every insult, every injury that will cause sorrow, that will cause disease in their body, that will cause their organs to cease to function, Father, I stop them in their tracks. I arrest them before they come and I say they shall not visit my children's temple, in the mighty name of Jesus.
40. My children's bodies are secure. My children's souls are secure. My children's spirits are secure, in the mighty name of Jesus. I will not have any reason to mourn concerning them. I will not have any reason to sorrow concerning my children. Lord, you will protect them - in the morning, in the afternoon and at night.

As you have declared, Lord I decree it is so.

CONCLUSION

Our Father and our God we thank you for this time of worship, we thank you for this hour in your presence. Thank you because you have heard us. Father, we stand upon this throne of mercy as mothers, we stand in the gap praying for our children; this is all we know to do.

Father even those who are yet to conceive who have joined in, Father, I ask oh Lord, that heaven will hear us in the name of Jesus. Father, every prayer point we have raised before you today, we receive answers to them in the name of Jesus.

Father Lord, some of us are laying foundations for their future, therefore, Father we ask, oh Lord, peradventure, the enemy decides to visit our children, You will lay remembrance upon this time of prayer today and your mercy will speak on their behalf.

We thank you because you have heard us. In Jesus name we have prayed.

Amen.

Chapter 7
REST AND REWARD OF MOTHERS

There is no doubt that most women labour to see their children succeed in life. We avoid luxuries and we deny ourselves pleasures, all for one purpose. That our children can have access to the very best.

Our expectation is that when the children are well established, they will remember all that we have done for them and love us and honour us for all that we have given up, for them to be where they are.

How much a woman will rest in her old age depends on what seeds are sown into her children's lives and their interpretation of the value added by their mother. . God expects us to experience old age and He expects it to be glorious.

> **Genesis 35: 16**
>
> *Then they moved on from Bethel. While they were still some distance from Ephrath, Rachel began to give birth and had great difficulty. 17 And as she was having great difficulty in childbirth, the midwife said to her, "Don't despair, for you have another son." 18 As she breathed her last—for she was dying—she named her son Ben-Oni.[h] But his father named him Benjamin.[i] 19 So Rachel died and was buried on the way to Ephrath (that is, Bethlehem). 20 Over her tomb Jacob set up a pillar, and to this day that pillar marks Rachel's tomb.*

We all know the story of JACOB AND RACHEL. The delay that Rachel had in child-rearing ....the torture from her sister Leah, the accusations.

Eventually, she gave birth to two great sons; Joseph and Benjamin. Joseph became a great man. One to be reckoned with, in the society. He went on and made his father's name popular and also do great and mighty work to establish his family. But then his mother had died. Of what use is all your effort when you are not able to enjoy the reward?

However there are factors that may affect this REST that we desire in our old age....

1. Ill health
2. Premature death
3. Children's perception of our help
4. Children's nuclear family
5. Powers beyond human control.

Today, we will be praying regarding these;
Ill health can be in any form ; Physical, mental etc. There are illnesses that make it impossible for people to help you.

1. Lord, I receive a sound mind from now till my old age. My intellect will function perfectly and I have a sharp mind, I am able to process information and understand events. Everything that I need to do now, to maintain my mind, lord, I receive the wisdom to do in Jesus name
2. Lord, the human body is designed to age as it grows, every ageing that happens in my body will be healthy ageing.
3. Diseases and illness will not find an expression within my body from now till my old age.
4. Every tissue, every cell in my body, I speak life to you today and

decree that you will serve me until the very end in Jesus name.
5. I receive correction for every abnormality that has started in my body, and I decree that you are stopped in your tracks right now. My body is designed to serve me till the very end, and this shall be the case.

Premature Death

We have all seen that life can be so unfair sometimes....whatever life has in mind, my contract with God is that I will enjoy the fruit of my labour.

1. Lord, I decree that I shall not die but live to see the goodness of the Lord in the lives of my children
2. I receive a long full and rewarding life, this is my entitlement as a child of God.
3. The Bible says that a workman is worthy of his wages, I am working hard and labouring for my children's future, when the time shall come for me to enjoy my labour, I shall not see corruption in Jesus name.
4. Every pre-existing contract that has been outlined to destroy me before the time of my joy, Lord, today, by your blood, I wipe them out permanently.
5. Lord, in my lifetime, my eyes shall not see any evil regarding my children. All the goodness that will cause my heart to rejoice in old age, so shall come my way and that of my children in Jesus name

Children's Perception.

1. Lord, When the time shall come for my children to take care of me, I ask that you will remind them of all that I have done and all my labour regarding them
2. I pray that my children will never take for granted all that I have done for them in life
3. In my old age, they will be merciful to me and help me
4. My head shall find a place of rest in my old age

5. My children shall be endued with all that is needful for them to care for me.

Children Spouses
1. Lord, every spouse that will turn my children against me in my old age, I ask that you send far away from them.
2. I have laboured and I deserve rest, every in law that will cause sorrow and distress for my children and deprive me of peace in my old age, Lord, I send far from them in the name of Jesus.

> **See what Proverbs 16:31(NASB) says:**
> A gray head is a crown of glory; it is found in the way of righteousness.

Grey hair is a sign of God's blessing; getting old is a blessing but not all old people are enjoying this old age. You will pray God's plan for your old age.

> **Psalm 23:1-6(MSG)**
> God, my shepherd! I don't need a thing. 1. Lord, you have directed my path through life; I decree that, in my moment of rest, nothing I need will be missing or wanting. 2. You have bedded me down in lush meadows.

Pray now and say:
1. Father, no man receives anything except they be given from above. receive a comfortable rest in my end; I decree a rest that is void of hardship.
2. **You find me quiet pools to drink from.** Father, you are the one who allocates people to quiet pools; you direct people to befitting lifestyles. Lord, direct my path towards a peaceful and rewarding end.

3. **True to your word, you let me catch my breath and send me in the right direction.** You know what lies ahead, Lord. Send me in the right direction for my future rest.
4. **Even when the way goes through Death Valley, I'm not afraid when you walk at my side. Your trusty shepherd's crook makes me feel secure.** Lord, the path ahead has many corners and bends. Lord, I hold on to you for my security and confidence.
5. **You serve me a six-course dinner right in front of my enemies.** Father, I am aware that there are many people who wait until the time of rest before they point accusing fingers. I give you permission to prosper me evidently before the eyes of they that despise me.
6. **You revive my drooping head.** Old age is a time when many are laden with diseases and problems. Lord, I receive renewal of vitality in my old age.
7. Diseases and infirmity will not hinder me from enjoying my labour upon my children.
8. **My cup brims with blessings.** For many, old age is the time of counting regrets. Lord, for me, it shall be a time of recounting God's great mercy towards me
9. As I grow old, everything around me shall remind me of God's faithfulness.

> *Job 36:7,11(NCV)*
> He always watches over those who do right; he sets them on thrones with kings and they are honoured forever. If they obey and serve him, the rest of their lives will be successful, and the rest of their years will be happy.

10. Father, I have served and obeyed you. According to your word, you will set me in great places in life and your eyes will watch over me persistently.
11. Father ,in my time of rest and reward, may honour never depart

from me.
12. The rest of my days will be successful.
13. The rest of my years will be spent in joy. Nothing shall hold back my joy in my time of rest.
14. He does not withdraw his eyes from the righteous, but with kings on the throne he sets them forever, and they are exalted. Lord, I declare that your eyes will persistently be upon me.
15. **Lord, your word says,** If they listen and serve him, they complete their days in prosperity, and their years in pleasantness. I have served and obeyed you, my days shall be completed in pleasantness

Job 36:7, 11 (ESV)
7. And he said, "My presence will go with you, and I will give you rest." 11. And the Lord said to Moses, "This very thing that you have spoken I will do, for you have found favour in my sight, and I know you by name."

Exodus 33:14, 17 (ESV)
16. Father, let your presence go ahead of me into my old age; I receive rest for the season. 17. You, Lord, give perfect peace to those who keep their purpose firm and put their trust in you. Lord, you make the path smooth for good people; the road they travel is level.

Isaiah 26:3, 7 (GNT)
18. Lord, you make the path smooth for me in my season of rest in old age.

Chapter 8
MOTHER HELPED BY GOD

In this section, we are going to spend some time praying for ourselves and also for our children. We are going to be praying for our children, both those in school, out of school or those going back to school soon. We shall spend some time praying for them, to commit them in the hands of God for the new year. We are also going to receive grace for all that we need, even to support these children through the new school year. So, I trust that as the Lord helps us through this; as we pray the will of God through concerning our children, in the name of Jesus.

I have thought about the challenge's women face while raising children. Some of the questions my daughter asks makes me wonder how she got that kind of wisdom and how on earth I can put the right words together to speak and to explain things. This is what we need in this day and age sisters; I'm sure most of you can identify with what this. Children are very challenging these days, they do not take No for an answer, they do not take Yes for an answer; they just want an explanation for everything. So, *what do we need?* As relevant mothers in this age, we need to be ready with answers.

I will share with you something I discovered about the story of Jesus and Mary; a biblical example where a son challenged the mother's decision or instruction. Jesus turned water into wine in this first miracle, the Bible says that there was a marriage; there was a wedding and Mary was there with Jesus. They ran out of wine at that wedding and Mary went to Jesus and Mary said, *"Jesus, they've ran out of wine."* The Bible says that Jesus looked at her mother and said, *"Woman, why are you bothering me? Why is it my business that they've ran out of wine?"* The Bible reports that when Jesus replied Mary that way, Mary turned around and walked away but she gave instructions to the disciples. And she told them, *"Whatever He tells you, do it."* There are times mothers you just need to walk away. A lot of shout at our children; we shout at them as though we are going to shout them into submission. No! We will be praying that the Lord will give us the wisdom. The wisdom, the same type Mary used on this occasion. That wisdom was just amazing, she knew what was right. She pushed Jesus towards what was right and then she let Him be.

We are therefore going to pray, ask God and say:
1. Lord, my child is unique. All my children are unique. Help me to get this motherhood business right with your help.

Mary did not start arguing with Jesus. She moved on and she made plans.

You are going to ask :
2. Lord give me wisdom for every situation, for every challenge that will come in dealing with my children. The Lord will give me wisdom in the mighty name of Jesus, to be able to answer my children. How to speak to them, how to address them, when to keep quiet, when to correct, when to encourage, when to support, when to be firm when to be soft, in the name of Jesus.
3. The Lord will give me instructions. Step by step instructions how to go about my responsibilities.
4. God please give me direction. He will give you the right wisdom. You may not respond to your children every time; you may not correct and tell them off all the time.
5. Lord, I am asking in the name of Jesus that you will give me insight. You will help me to know when to respond and when to be quiet. This is my prayer Lord, in the mighty of Jesus.
6. Lord, my children are unique. Father, they have a unique destiny. I

cannot compare them one to another neither can I compare them to other children. Father, I am asking Lord in the mighty name of Jesus, for unique grace to carry out my unique task.
7. *All I will need oh Lord, to be an excellent mum as I support them....they will be asking me questions about different challenges they are facing. Father I am asking in the name of Jesus, for insight and for wisdom, to speak a word in season, in the mighty name of Jesus.*
8. *Father, I receive insight into your solutions for every situation ahead of them this year, in Jesus name.*

I shared with some people the question my son asked me a question a while back. My son said, "You know everybody is having a girlfriend; they are all having girlfriends, Mom. What is happening how do I say to them that I don't want a girlfriend?" I said, "Now, let's talk about what a girlfriend is. Let's talk about why you do not need a girlfriend for now." So, I took him through a few things, and I said, "you enjoy ballet a few years ago, now, you don't enjoy it anymore. This happened only in a few years; you will not even have any time for it in the next few years. Your choice will also be different, your taste will change; your likes would be different."

I'm sure a lot of us, are not in a position to answer questions for our children, you dismiss them, and you say, "What nonsense? As a child of God, you're not allowed to do that..." You need to be able to meet them at the point where they can understand.

So, you are going to ask the lord:
9. Lord, put a word in my mouth for my children, put a word that would minister to them. It is not every word that would minister to them. Father give me the right words to speak to them. Father give me the

right words to impact wisdom to them, in the mighty name of Jesus.
10. *I receive for myself, Father Lord God Almighty, insight, wisdom to speak the language they will understand, in the mighty name of Jesus.*
11. *My children will not turn their back against God because of their instruction and the advice I gave them. Not because of my parenting skills oh Lord, in the mighty name of Jesus.*
12. *Father Lord God Almighty, there is no way they can stand, Father Lord God Almighty, faced with opposition and the questions from their colleagues, not having a strong base. Father I am asking Lord, in the name of Jesus, for the wisdom for me to be able to lead them in a strong foundation. Father, in the name of Jesus.*
13. *Instruct them in your word oh Lord and help them apply it to their lives the way they will understand, in the mighty name of Jesus. This is my desire, Lord. In Jesus name.*

Every child is different, some need to be made to sit down in one place without a smack; another only needs eye contact; but at times we do not know what method to use.

You're going to pray, and you are going to ask the Lord and say:
14. Lord, you made these children. You designed them in the womb. Before I saw them at all, you knew them. Help me discover how to help them.
15. You are going to ask the Lord, to lead you, teach you and to show you who your children are, in the name of Jesu
16. Say father, reveal to me who my children are. Reveal to me who you've given to me to take care of. Reveal to me the destinies that you have given unto me, in the name of Jesus.

17. Father open my eyes to understand the right principles of life to govern them by. That I may be able to apply the right principles of the scripture to them in the mighty name of Jesus. That I will not mislead them. That I will not misguide them, in the mighty name of Jesus.

Parenting can be very tedious, watching parent talk with their teenager children always seem the world is coming to an end. Most especially If there were not present when his children were growing and did not have a relationship with them.

You are going to pray, and you are going to say:
18. Lord, I don't want to lose my mind. Father preserve my mind so that I will be in the right frame of mind to address and to instruct my teenagers; to address and to instruct my children as they grow.

Some things four-year-old's say some sometimes make you think "Goodness Gracious, how did that come out of your mouth?"

Pray that the:
19. Lord will preserve your mind. Your mind will be sound in the name of Jesus. You will not be confused. You will not be distracted. You will have the right information at the right time to supply these children, in the mighty name of Jesus.
20. Father, I pray Lord, Father for the right word at the right time for my children, in the name of Jesus. That I will know how to speak. That I will know how to answer them, in the name of Jesus, word of wisdom that will impact on to their lives positively. In the mighty name of Jesus. This is what I desire, Jesus. This is what I pray for my

children in the name of Jesus.

I was reading about Rebecca through Genesis 27; a story I know many of you have read many times. In his old age, Jacob called Esau his oldest son and said to him *"give me something to eat."* Rebecca their mother heard that conversation; she made haste and passed the message across to her favourite son and do you know what? The generations were never the same after that because a mother lacked wisdom. Your children's schools may contact you to complain about your child's behaviour; sometimes it may the neighbors who contacts you, calls your attention to their observation of your children, or what they have noticed about your child.

You are going to pray:
21. *For wisdom to be able to sift the truth from deception so that you will not punish your children unjustly and so that you will not be offended by the instruction that will be coming from outside.*
22. *I believe that the Lord is raising this prayer point specifically for some parents. Every time the teacher calls you, you take a fight to the school. Every time somebody says something, you go and defend your child. What is the Lord saying about that situation? you need wisdom to handle it, Receive it now, in Jesus name.*

There are times when your immediate correction saves a child's life.

You are going to pray tonight and say:
23. *Lord, wherever the correction is coming from, Father, I receive insight. Father give me insight so I will know when to speak, when to fight and when to correct my children, in the name of Jesus.*
24. *My choices will not lead to their downfall, in the mighty name of*

Jesus. My choices will not destroy my children's life, in the mighty name of Jesus.

25. *Father Lord God Almighty, you will send school authority, you will send neighbors, you will send church members, you will send my friends. You will send people I can trust – people I can listen to when it is time to pay attention to particular things in my children's life, in the mighty name of Jesus.*
26. *I will hear clearly. Father, I receive a discerning spirit to know when they are saying the truth, when I need to act and when I need to be quiet, in the mighty name of Jesus. Father,*
27. *I receive express insight, express discernment, in the name of Jesus regarding my children and their career; Father Lord God Almighty, I will know who to believe, I will know who to trust in the judgement concerning my children in the name of Jesus.*

I see many parents getting agitated during school resumption seasons; some of the message are like, *"Omobola, pray my daughter is going to secondary school for the first time."* We need to keep in mind that, *Except the lord builds the house, except the lord watches over the house, they labour in vain who stay awake at night.* You're going to pray, as many of you whose children are going into new schools, your children are going to new classes, they're going to be on the new teachers they are going to be under new headmasters or even they are going to the university.

You are going to say, Lord:

28. *I release my children to you; I will not stay awake at night worrying over them because you will take care of them. You made them; you preserved them in the womb when I could not reach them; when there was nothing, I could do than to wait in expectation for the ninth month. Father, I release my children to you. I hand them over to you. You are able to preserve them. You said you are able to keep whatever that has been committed into your care in Jesus name.*

Lord, I ask regarding my children, I commit them into your care Oh Lord, in the name of Jesus.

29. In the new academic year, Lord you will watch over them. You preserve them. No evil will come near them. No evil shall befall them, in the mighty name of Jesus.
30. In the morning when they wake up, your eyes will be upon them. In the afternoon when they are at school, your eyes will be upon them. When they return at night, your eyes will be upon them. In the mighty name of Jesus.
31. You will preserve them day in day out, in the name of Jesus. Every day of this year, my heart will be rested in your assurance oh Lord of protection for my children Lord, in the name of Jesus.
32. You will preserve them as they go to school, as they are at school, as they come back from school, when they come back home, whilst they are at home, while they sleep at night, in the name of Jesus.

The Bible says in Psalm 112, "they will not be afraid of bad news. Their hearts are steady. They are confident and they will not be afraid."

We are going to pray that prayer again, you are going to say:
33. Lord I refuse to be afraid of bad news regarding my children as they step out. I shall not be afraid of bad news because it will not come to me regarding my children, in the mighty name of Jesus.
34. Bad news will not come to me regarding my children in the name of Jesus. Not from the teacher at school, not from the health services, not from any caregiver even not from the nanny, not from the after-school club, in the mighty name of Jesus.
35. I shall not be afraid of bad news because my heart trusts in you, in the mighty name of Jesus.
36. Father, your protection is a reliable one. Your protection is a worthy one. Father, I ask on this Lord, for this new year, my children are trusting in you. Father, you will preserve them, in the mighty name of Jesus.

A while ago we were studying the book of Kings on the Shunammite woman. She had one child whose birth was miraculous; The Bible says that, that boy left home and went with his father to the field and developed a sudden headache; they brought him to his father who said, *"Take him back to his mother."*

We are going to be pray and say:
37. Lord, regarding my children in this new school year, I will not receive a phone call to attend emergency. I will not receive a phone call to attend hospital. I will not receive a phone call to come and identify any dead body, in the mighty name of Jesus.
38. Regarding my children, Father, I shall not receive any sad news concerning them. I will not be afraid of it and it shall not come to me, in the mighty name of Jesus.
39. Father Lord God Almighty, for my children, I decree, and I declare Lord I shall not receive bad news regarding them Father Lord God Almighty, the Shunamite woman - the Bible says, the boy went out with his father to the field and developed a sudden sickness. I say, I cancel, and I reject every sudden illness every sudden sickness that will make my children to become invalid and will be running helter skelter looking for my contact details. Every accident at school that will make them to be looking for my number in case of emergency, Father, I reject in the name of Jesus.
40. I preserve my children away from all harm, away from all evil, in the mighty name of Jesus.
41. Disaster will not visit them. Calamity will not visit them. They are preserved as they go out. They're preserved as they come in the mighty name of Jesus.

We're going to pray against every outbreak of diseases and every epidemic. We are going to pray that our children shall be safe from all these. We need to keep in mind that the devil has not stopped designing and fashioning new diseases. A while ago in Nigeria it was said that rats were passing diseases to humans. At some point they said it was Lassa fever. They said it was Ebola virus. You're going to pray. How can you keep your children, you cannot keep them except they do not meet people?

You are going to pray and say:
42. My children, I secure you from every outbreak of diseases, from every epidemic. I decree you shall be safe in the mighty name of Jesus.
43. Whatever is killing many, will not kill you. Whatever is infecting many, will not infect you. Whatever is infesting many, will not infest you. I decree in the mighty name of Jesus.
44. I put the banner of the Lord over you, in the mighty name of Jesus. I decree you are preserved from every epidemic, from every disaster, from every calamity, from every destruction that waste at noonday in the mighty name of Jesus.
45. In the name of Jesus, I infuse you with the power of the living God, with the blood of Jesus and I decree your immunity shall break every hold of diseases, in the mighty name of Jesus.
46. I infuse your blood and your body with the life of Christ, in the name of Jesus. I immunize you with the blood of Jesus today, my children, against every infestation and infection, in the mighty name of Jesus.
47. I decree you are secure, and you are guarded, away from all the infirmity away from illnesses and sicknesses, in Jesus name.

We are going to pray regarding what these children eat and drink.

You're going to play and say:
48. My children you will not be poisoned, you will not be contaminated in the mighty name of Jesus.

Children pick all sorts of things to eat in school; I heard a story long ago, how a child tasted one of their friend's food in school; she ate the part that had gone off and that was the beginning of calamity.

We are going to pray tonight and say:
49. Lord my children, I'm not there to supervise them; whatsoever goes into their mouth will preserve them, it will not destroy them. They will not be poisoned, they will not be contaminated by what goes into their mouth, in the name of Jesus.
50. Whether it be food, whether it be drink in the name of Jesus, diseases shall not invade their body by the reason of what goes into their mouth in the name of Jesus.
51. Father, I secure my children, Lord God Almighty, everything that will go into their mouth, be it school dinner, be it food from friends, be it drinks when they go on school trips, in the name of Jesus.
52. I secure and I preserve them from contamination, from poisoning, in Jesus name.

We are going to pray once again against every devilish association. Another story I hears talks about some children who went on a school trip, not knowing that the hall that they were visiting, was enchanted. That was how a little boy picked a toy from the floor and it was the start of a diseases that the none could not explain.

You are going to decree and declare:
53. As my children go out to school, whatever they will come in contact with, I reject and I refuse every devilish association, in the mighty name of Jesus.
54. My children will not put their hands on things that will contaminate them spiritually in the mighty name of Jesus.
55. I refuse and I reject every spiritual contamination of my children by the reason of contact, by the reason of visit, in the name of Jesus.
56. Every devilish association, every devilish contract, in the name of Jesus, I cancel, and I reject. In the mighty name of Jesus.
57. I secure you my children. I secure your borders. I say spiritually, you

shall be fortified, in the name of Jesus, from every penetration of the enemy of your spirit, from evil forces in the name of Jesus.

We are going to pray right now.
    The Bible says in Psalm 119:99: *I have become smarter than my teachers because I have pondered and absorbed your counsel.*
    There is a wisdom a child has that baffles the teacher, stands the children out and makes the teachers refer to them when they cannot understand subject matters. That is supernatural wisdom.

You are going to pray and say:
58. Lord, I decree concerning my children, regarding this academic year, my children I decree your wisdom is greater than that of your teachers in the mighty name of Jesus. Whatever they find unable to unravel, the Lord will give you, insight, in the mighty name of Jesus.
59. You will stand out in excellence. You will do better and above your mates, in the mighty name of Jesus.

There is something called outstanding performance in the UK.

60. Decree and declare that your children shall stand out not just among their peers but outstanding everywhere and in all areas, in the mighty name of Jesus.
61. They shall excel, they shall be seen far above, in the name of Jesus. Only the great and mighty places in life is befitting for our children.
62. Father I decree regarding my children Lord God Almighty; I see excellence in the way they will stand out, in the mighty name of Jesus.
63. Father Lord God Almighty, when everybody is standing at the same level, my children will stand tall, high and far above them, in a distinguishable manner, in the mighty name of Jesus.

One of the things we need to keep remembering is that, if you cannot afford school fees, it is a frustration that can stop your children, no matter how excellent they are.

You are going to ask for supernatural help:
64. The finance you need to train these children, that the Lord will release help to you, in the mighty name of Jesus.
65. Supernatural sustenance for this new academic year. Before the need arises, the Lord will raise help. Before the need arises, the Lord will open doors. Before the need arises, the Lord will send help. Financial help will come. Psychological help will come, in the mighty name of Jesus.
66. In this new academic year, the Lord will send me helpers, in the mighty name of Jesus. Help will arise for me. Father Lord God Almighty, whatever is needed for my children to excel at school, father whether it is in the form of money, whether it is in the form of personnel, Father I receive it Lord, in the mighty name of Jesus.
67. My children will not lack any good thing in this new academic year. In Jesus name.

We are going to pray for their class teachers, you are going to pray for as many people as will be teaching your children. Please understand that a mad teacher can only impact madness into the children.

You are going to pray for the teachers teaching your children; say to them:
68. Teachers, I decree a sound mind for you, in the mighty name of Jesus. You will not impact unto my children the wrong lessons. You will not teach my children the wrong things. You will not pass negative thoughts and negative lifestyle to my children, in the mighty name of Jesus.
69. As many teachers as the devil has contracted to destroy by the reason of wrong doctrines, in the name of Jesus, I cancel your

appointment with my children's school. I say it shall not stand in the mighty name of Jesus.
70. Because my children are in that school, we decree and we declare that prosperity and righteousness shall be the portion of the school and the class in which my children will seat, in the mighty name of Jesus.
71. The board of government for the school, in the name of Jesus will make right laws. In the name of Jesus, they will pass the right counsel regarding the school, regarding everything that will happen at the school. Everything that will affect my children, I decree Lord, the judgement shall be righteous, in the mighty name of Jesus.

There are times when the class teacher picks on a child and decides that the child is going to suffer. When I was in the secondary school and in the university days, if you happen to have a lecturer who likes you sexually and you refuse, you are in trouble. You will be repeating year after year. They failed you course after course. That in another word these days is called bullying and victimization.

You are going to pray because the Bible says that the chastisement of our peace has been laid upon the Lord Jesus Christ.

You are going to decree:
72. That your children will be free from bullying. They will be free from victimization, in the mighty name of Jesus.

Some children, they keep changing schools, whatever new school they go to, they are bullied, whatever new school they go to, they don't find friend.

You are going to pray and say Lord:
73. I decree concerning my children. My children shall not be bullied, my children shall not be victimized in the mighty name of Jesus. The

Bible says, let no man trouble me, for I bear upon my body the marks of Christ. I put the mark of Christ upon my son, upon my daughter. I frustrate every hand that raises against you unduly, any hand that raises itself to punish you, any hand that raises itself to cause you distress, in the mighty name of Jesus.

74. *I decree in the mighty name of Jesus, in your school year, in your place of work or business, peace shall be your portion in the mighty name of Jesus. You shall not be troubled, you shall not be distressed, in the mighty name of Jesus. No adult shall seek to harm you.*
75. *No child, no adult shall succeed in their bid to hurt you, in the mighty name of Jesus. This shall be the case every morning, every afternoon, every nighttime, in the mighty name of Jesus.*
76. *Say you have decreed, and you have declared that your children will not be victims of any form of harassment or punishment in this season and in times to come, in the name of Jesus.*

The position where a child seats in class is important; the room they are allocated in the university is important. We are going to pray tonight. The bible says that *the lines are falling onto us in pleasant places.*

You are going to decree:

77. *My children as you go to class, the lines are falling onto you in pleasant places. The choice of who sits on your right, the choice of who will sit on your left, the choice of where you sit in the class, the choice of whose class you are going to be sitting in, the choice of who is going to be a moderator, the choice of who is going to be your head of year, the choice of which hostel you are going to be allocated, the choice of which hostel you are going to be in, the choice of the roommates you will have.*
78. *I decree and declare the bible says that the lines are falling unto me in pleasant places. I decree concerning my children and I said whatever allocation has been made unto you in this new academic year, it is a pleasant place for you to flourish. It is a pleasant place*

for you to prosper in the mighty name of Jesus.
79. *You will prosper as you get there you will prosper as you are sustained, in the mighty name of Jesus.*
80. *The expectation of the lord upon you shall not be cut short in this academic year, in the mighty name of Jesus. In Jesus name.*

This is the last prayer point for this chapter. I have seen so many situations where children have seemingly innocent accidents and their lives are turned around negatively afterwards.

We are going to pray:
81. *My Children, this new academic year, you will not break a bone. This new academic year, you will not face any disaster. This new academic year no other child will hurt or harm you. This new academic year no vehicle will knock you down. This new academic year you will not face any calamity.*
82. *This new academic year, the Lord will give you a righteous possession. This new academic year, peace shall be your portion. This new academic year, you will excel beyond expectation this new academic year, disease shall not visit your habitation.*
83. *The Bible says in **Psalm 34:7**. It says on every side, the Lord's messenger protects everyone who honours God and delivers them. I assign guardian angels to you my children on every side. If the evil is coming from above, it will miss you. If it comes from below, you will miss it. If it is coming from the front, you'd have gone. If it is coming from the back, it will not catch up with you, in the mighty name of Jesus. If it is coming from the right from the left, you shall be secure, in the mighty name of Jesus.*

The bible says that the angels of the Lord encamps around those that fear Him and delivers them.
84. *I decree in the name of Jesus throughout this academic year my children, the angels of the Lord - they encompass around you and*

they deliver you from every calamity, from every evil, from every disaster. Father, we give you praise because you have heard us in Jesus name.

CONCLUSION

Our Father and our God, we want to thank you for tonight. Thank you, lord, because you always hear us. We can only pray as much as we know how to pray. The Bible says that we should redeem the times for the days are evil. Father, we come together as a body of parents and we want to commit our children on to you as they start the new academic year. We pray for ourselves first oh Lord, whatever wisdom is needed for this new year; whatever wisdom is needed for this new school season, Father as mothers we receive in Jesus name.

Lord in the name of Jesus. Father, we want to ask specifically, for the grace and the patience to pay attention to our children. At times our children are going through things, they do not even know how to talk to us. Some of us parents are so busy with so many things, we do not have the time to listen. Father, I am asking for myself and all the parents who are connected to this prayer time that you will wake us up and you will bring us to a halt when something is happening, and we need to be alert.

Father, wake ourselves from our slumber to stop us in our tracks oh Lord when we need to pay attention to our children, in Jesus name; Father, we pray especially for our children Father, the ones who are going to the nursery, who are going to primary school, who are going to secondary school, who are in the university, who are entering the university... we pray for the new ones oh Lord, they're going into new territories. Father, we are sending your word ahead of them. We say Lord God Almighty that you will give ground to flourish wherever they go in the name of Jesus. Father, we say they shall not be afraid. They will go with boldness and you will encompass them with favour as a shield in the name of Jesus.

Father we secure our children from every harm, from every infection, from infestation, from calamity, from disaster in the mighty name of Jesus. We secure them from every epidemic; we say evil that is coming will *not catch up with them, Father Lord God Almighty, they will not catch up with evil. Father, we decree concerning their teachers and their classmates, we say Lord God Almighty, the steps of the righteous the bible says, are ordered of God. Father our children's steps are ordered. Peradventure, they've been allocated to wrong classes and wrong teachers, Father we start to decree a rearrangement spiritually that will come into physical manifestation in the name of Jesus. Father Lord, we have committed these children unto you, and we decree that in this academic year, our children are only permitted to be above and never below. We receive for them the spirit of excellence. We receive for them wisdom that is more than that of their teachers, in the name of Jesus. The Bible says I'm as wonder unto many but you oh Lord, are my confidence. Father, we decree concerning our children, this shall be their testimonies. In this academic year, they shall be a wonder to their teachers, to their colleagues, in the name of Jesus. Because you oh Lord will be their strength. Father, we thank you because you have heard us. We have you glory and honour Lord, in Jesus name we have prayed.*

Amen!

Chapter 9
MERCY

God designed mercy as withhold punishment from they who deserve it. No one can understand mercy as a parent. Your child does wrong and you know that you don't want them to cry but you still need to correct them, so they don't miss it in life. God is the father of mercy; whatever little mercy you feel as a parent, it's just a little percentage of God's mercy. Mercy is His nature and He gives us just a little of it.

There are spiritual rules and once you trigger the cascade, it keeps going. If you break the edge, the serpent will bite. The enemy is quick to accuse, but we know better; we have the advantage for we are already in a covenant. Let's see:

> ***1 Kings 11:9-13(CEVDC):***
> *9-10 The Lord God of Israel had appeared to Solomon two times and warned him not to worship foreign gods. But Solomon disobeyed and did it anyway. This made the Lord very angry, **11** and he said to Solomon: You did what you wanted and not what I told you to do. Now I'm going to take your kingdom from you and give it to one of your officials. **12** But because David was your father, you will remain king as long as you live. I will wait until your son becomes king, then I will take the kingdom from him. **13** When I do, I will still let him rule one tribe, because I have not forgotten that David was my servant and Jerusalem is my chosen city.*

Pray and say:
1. *The provision for your mercy has been made in the blood of Jesus by whom I have been saved. By reason of birth, I extend this same cover to my children; I decree that they will work before you and be*

perfect.

2. *Lord, I obtain your mercy for the present stage of my children's lives.*
3. *I obtain your mercy to cover them for years to come.*
4. *Lord, regarding my generation, I enter a covenant of mercy with you today and I agree with you that my children will stay under your care.*

> ### Job 1:4-5(MSG)
> **4-5** *His sons used to take turns hosting parties in their homes, always inviting their three sisters to join them in their merrymaking. When the parties were over, Job would get up early in the morning and sacrifice a burnt offering for each of his children, thinking, "Maybe one of them sinned by defying God inwardly."*

Job made a habit of this sacrificial atonement, just in case they'd sinned.

5. *I obtain mercy for every wrong word; every wrong action every disobedience to your words and instruction by my children.*
6. *I obtain your mercy to cover my children from the consequences of innocent utterances which are meant to lead to serious consequences.*
7. *I obtain mercy from God regarding His instructions to you, my children.*
8. *I obtain mercy from all men and women, instead of punishment, your wrongs shall be overlooked my children.*

Job covered his children; what he did was to pre-order God's mercy, so the enemy will not find a foothold to attack.

9. Lord, I pre-order a favourable decision for my children even before they do wrong.

> **Lamentations 3:22 (CJB)**
> That the grace of ADONAI* is not exhausted, that his compassion has not ended. [23] [On the contrary,] they are new every morning! How great your faithfulness!

There are reasons to be consumed daily, there is consumption on the street, in the air, even at home.

10. Lord, I speak your mercy upon my children, to preserve them from being consumed. I travelled on an international flight recently and a young man was being harassed. The woman started making declarations and proclamations.
11. Lord, I obtain mercy in advance for every error and ungodly altercation that may involve my children.
12. I say that the wicked one will find it impossible to punish them.

> **Psalms 57:1 (NLT)**
> 1 Have mercy on me, O God, have mercy! I look to you for protection. I will hide beneath the shadow of your wings until the danger passes by. He will send help from heaven to rescue me, disgracing those who hound me. Interlude My God will send

forth his unfailing love and faithfulness.

13. Lord, because of your mercy, protect my children.
14. Let your mercy speak for my children when destruction is around. Let it be obvious to all that it is your mercy that saved them.
15. Lord by your mercy, send help from heaven, to preserve my children until evil has passed.

> ### Daniel 9:9 (CJB)
> [9] It is for Adonai* our God to show compassion and forgiveness, because we rebelled against him.

> ### Psalms 86:15-16(KJV)
> 15 But thou, O Lord, art a God full of compassion, and gracious, longsuffering, and plenteous in mercy and truth. 16 O turn unto me and have mercy upon me; give thy strength unto thy servant and save the son of thine handmaid.

In the early years of THYORECIOUSJEWELS, God asked me for a jewel, I sent her a Facebook message immediately; *Where are you, I asked?* She replied, "Omob, please pray for me now." She had been kidnapped whilst working as a prostitute.

> ### Exodus 33:19 CEVDC
> 19 The Lord answered: All right. I am the Lord, and I show mercy and kindness to anyone I choose. I will let you see my glory and hear my holy name.

16. Lord let my children experience your mercy
17. Lord let my husband experience your mercy
18. Lord let me experience your mercy.
19. I obtain mercy in advance , for when they will cry to you for help in their time of need. I am thankful in advance for what you have done. In Jesus name I have prayed.

Printed in Great Britain
by Amazon